Rainbow
of Rhinestone Jewelry

— Lynn Ann Russell
Sandy Fichtner—

With Price Guide and Repairing Suggestions

Schiffer
Publishing Ltd

77 Lower Valley Road, Atglen, PA 19310

Dedication

We dedicate this effort to our friendship and common interest, which enabled the book to become a reality!

Library of Congress Cataloging-in-Publication data

Fichtner, Sandy.
Rainbow of rhinestone jewelry /
Sandy Fichtner and Lynn Ann Russell.
p. cm.--(A Schiffer book for collectors)
Includes bibliographical references and index.
ISBN 0-88740-895-8 (paper)
1. Rhinestone jewelry.
I. Russell, Lynn Ann. II. Title. III. Series.
NK4890.R48F53 1995
688'.2'075--dc20   95-37216
CIP

Printed in Hong Kong

Published by Schiffer Publishing Ltd.
77 Lower Valley Road
Atglen, PA 19310
Please write for a free catalog.
This book may be purchased from the publisher.
Please include $2.95 for shipping.
Try your bookstore first.

Contents

Introduction
Care of Your Collection

Rhinestone jewelry. To some it is full of wonder and awe, to others it is throw-away junk. If it were truly junk, would it have survived decades? Would it have brought such pleasure to so many? How many Christmas mornings, anniversaries, and birthdays were made brighter by these singularly brilliant gifts?

We began our collections on opposite coasts, in different decades, and for different reasons. We met in Oregon and began crossing paths at local garage sales, flea markets, and antique shows. We always seemed to be admiring the piece the other was wearing. Soon we were scouring the countryside together. Amazingly, we have never had a serious conflict over a discovered treasure. Our separate love for these pieces of the past brought us together and created a lasting friendship and now, a partnership.

Books such as this contain a wealth of information. Short of physically examining a piece, the photographs offer many clues to designer and age. Every time the pages are scanned, something new will be discovered. It is suggested that one pay particular attention to the form, settings, and depth of stones used in each piece. What seems overwhelming in the beginning will become second nature as you progress.

The history of costume jewelry is as wide and varied as the colors used to create it, only the imagination of the designer establishes boundaries.

As you will learn as you delve deeper into this craft, each designer had a "special something" they could be identified with. Eisenberg for their spectacular stones of endless depth; Miriam Haskell for the use of beads, wire, and detail; Hollycraft for their multitude of tiny paste set stones; HAR for the sometimes bizarre figural designs; Weiss for color and depth of stones; Schreiner for the reverse set stones; and so on.

It's always a challenge to try to identify a piece before you actually examine it. We have all been fooled now and again. Only time, trial, and error can train the eye to discern the true designer.

If you are reading this book, your goal is most likely to find a picture of something you already own or would like to add to your collection. It's always a thrill to discover your piece is just part of a set. Now the search is on!

We offer cleaning, repairing, and storage instructions, all of which cannot be stressed enough. Your care after purchase will determine the life and beauty of your precious treasures.

The most important single thing we want to impress is HAVE FUN. This jewelry was created for fun and has been serving that purpose for many, many years. Even when your collection becomes serious, never lose sight of the fun you can have admiring and wearing your wonderful pieces!

With that in mind, we leave you with a single thought - HAPPY HUNTING!

Price Guide

The values given are simply a guideline. Condition, quality, location, and demand can create great variables in these prices. Our research was done on both the West and East coasts and the prices reflect a median range of the two.

Chapter 1
Cleaning

This phase of caring for the rhinestone jewelry cannot be stressed enough! To be done correctly, it will take time and patience.

To begin, gather all the needed tools. The following list should help you get started (Fig. 1):

Note pad and pencil
Glass bowl (small)
Alcohol
Tweezers
Needle nose pliers
Several soft cloths
Towel
Soft toothbrush
Toothpicks
Jewelers Loupe (10 x)
Magnifying glass
   (table attached model)

The steps are simple but should not be hurried. After all, you may be dealing with decades of dust and buildup. Even though rhinestones may appear to be very sturdy, their sensitivity to temperature change is quite amazing. Handle with care. Never, ever submerge or dip a piece of costume jewelry!

Scrutinize the piece through the magnifying glass and/or loupe. This is a good time to tighten loose prongs or close O-rings. Make a note of more involved repairs to be dealt with later.

Pour a small amount of alcohol in the dish or bowl. Hold the piece UPSIDE DOWN. This will keep the moisture from getting behind the stones and destroying the foil backing which is the basis for the sparkle, clarity, and depth. Dip the toothbrush in the alcohol and tap on the edge of the dish to remove any excess. With the piece UPSIDE DOWN, gently brush the stones and crevices (Fig. 2). This is actually more of a massaging motion. Lay the piece UPSIDE DOWN on the spread towel to dry. Continue this process until all pieces are done. Allow about ten minutes for drying. Again, with the magnifying glass, examine each piece. If you have missed some area, repeat the process. Four or five times is not unusual for this. (Occasionally, stubborn buildup may have to be removed with the aid of a BIT of non-foaming ammonia. This should be done exactly as with the alcohol, but with extreme care.)

You may want to do each piece completely, not waiting for the drying step. Don't! Every time the piece is turned upright when damp, moisture may seep in and possibly create a dead stone.

The toothpicks and tweezers are used for buildup or lint removal. Use with care as a stone can easily be dislodged.

Your new piece should be treated with the care deserving such a treasure. It cannot be over emphasized how important this is. A wonderful piece has often been destroyed simply by trying to hurry this process.

Now, we have a question for you. Has anyone discovered a safe method for removing the green patina, usually caused by dampness? We've tried many techniques, all of which either damage the stones or the metal itself. No matter how many years we've been collecting, there are always some things that elude us.

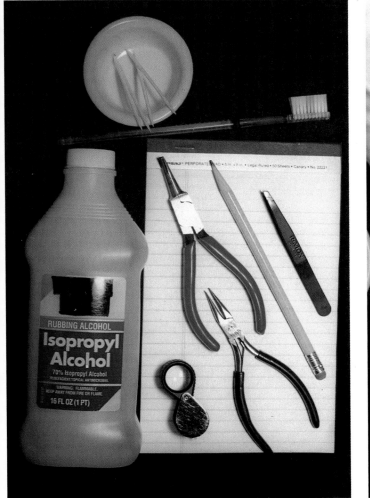

Fig. 1

Fig. 2

Chapter 2
Repairing

There are several places that specialize in the repair of costume jewelry, be it a break or missing stone. We choose to do as much as possible ourselves. Not only do we enjoy knowing every inch of the completed piece, but also that it has been done the way we prefer.

It is never too early to start collecting a variety of loose stones and findings (clasps, O-rings, etc.) for future repairs. Do not pass up any piece that is broken or has some missing stones if the remaining stones are of good quality, preferably prong set. Glued stones are difficult to remove with the foil backing intact. Never purchase a piece in need of repair unless you are certain you can repair it easily or need the stones. It is a good idea to collect several screw top containers for your loose stones. Thus, when repair pieces are found, the stones can be removed immediately and placed in these containers by color to be easily accessed when needed. If the piece to be used is signed, we prefer to leave the stones in until needed. In some cases, stones by a certain maker stand apart from others.

Now you are ready to begin. Having these tools at the ready will make your task simpler (Fig. 1):

SMALL screwdrivers
Toothpicks
Tweezers
Assortment of dental tools (if available)
Small needle nose pliers (2)
Screw top containers
Glue (Epoxy 330)
Non-porous dish or tin
Paper towels
Soft cloths
Jewelers Loupe (10x)
Magnifying glass
   (table attached and hand held)

Before proceeding, let us discuss the glues available. Epoxy 330 seems to be the best for this purpose. It does not harm the foil back and sets rapidly. Although it does require mixing, it is better to waste some than to use an inferior substance. All-purpose household cement does not stand up over the long term and is not as durable.

An invaluable tool is the lighted magnifying glass which attaches to the table. It enables cleaning, repairing, etc., up close with free hands. At about $20, it is an inexpensive addition and will be used constantly. No serious collector should be without one.

In this chapter we will attempt to give you step by step instructions on simple repairs. Patience is the key.

Replacing Stones

When it is discovered there is a missing or dead stone--one which no longer has its sparkle caused by dampness, age, or mistreatment (Fig. 2)--the first step is to scour your replacement stone containers for the closest match (Fig. 3.) A "brother or sister" stone (one of the same depth, clarity, and approximate age) is best. Make sure the foil back is completely intact or your effort will have undesirable results.

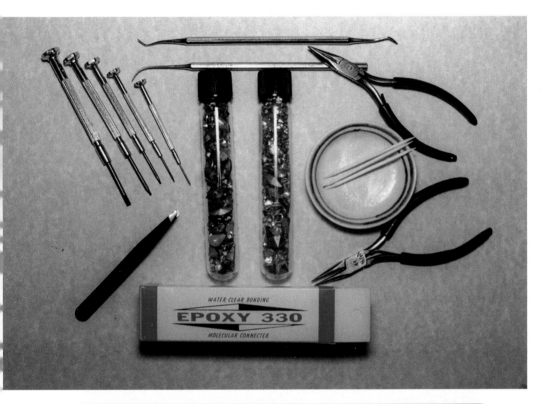

Fig. 1

Fig. 2

Fig. 3

Fig. 4

In the case of paste set stones, examine the stone for glue particles or other debris. Clean if necessary. Using a toothpick or dental pick, remove any buildup from the area the new stone is to be mounted in. Mix the glue. It is always better to mix up too much than not enough. Break off one end of a toothpick. With the sharp end, dip in the glue and apply a **SMALL** amount in the vacant area (Fig. 4.) Using the broken end, dab out any excess (a wooden golf tee works great too.) Depending on your dexterity, use either your fingers or the tweezers to place the stone (Fig. 5.) Should there be any excess glue around the newly placed stone, remove it immediately. If you have removed as much as possible prior to setting the stone, this should not be a problem. It is a good idea to practice on an inferior piece, removing and gluing stones, as this entire process becomes easier with practice.

If the stone you are replacing is prong set, the process is much simpler. After locating the correct replacement stone, GENTLY straighten the prongs of the piece you are working on. Center the new stone in the space and push the prongs GENTLY over the stone. Do not use a metal tool for this as it may scratch the stone. Any wood or plastic object may be used or there are prong tools available at craft and jewelry supply stores.

Fig. 5

Fig. 6

Replacing O-rings

An O-ring is the small circular metal piece that will either connect the necklace, bracelet, etc., to the clasp or suspend a "drop" from a chain. Many times with wear, an O-ring will be lost. Sometimes you will even discover a wonderful piece at a much reduced price simply because the O-ring is missing. This is one of the simplest repairs to do so do not pass this bargain up.

To match an O-ring, attention must be paid to color and age. There are many shades of gold and silver. Once the correct match is found, use two pairs of small needle nose pliers to open it. With pliers on either side of the ring separation, GENTLY twist one plier towards you and the other away (Fig. 6.) Do not go any farther than necessary. Never pull the ring apart. This greatly weakens the metal. Still holding the ring with one plier, use the other hand to remove or add the attachment. Once this is accomplished, use the pliers to GENTLY twist the ring closed in the same manner as opened. Be sure that there is no gap remaining in the O-ring to catch during wear.

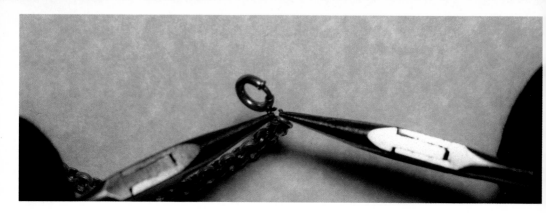

Fig. 7

Replacing spring clasps

A spring clasp may be used on either necklaces or bracelets. When the nodule is pulled back, the clasp opens and when released it closes, one part inserting into the other. When these break they cannot be repaired and must be replaced.

Replacement is accomplished by spreading the small circle at the base of the spring clasp (Fig. 7.), much the same as with the O-ring. Care must be taken not to separate the ring too much, weakening the connection. Again, be sure the colors are as close as possible.

Fig. 8

Replacing fold-over clasps

Fold-over clasps come in all sizes and are used primarily on necklaces and bracelets. When open, one end is inserted through the opposite end of the piece, then "folded over." Replacing these can be tricky. Should the clasp be bent too much in removal, it will not fit back together properly. Practice is the key.

Open the clasp. The attached clasp wraps around the end of the bracelet or necklace. Using a dental tool, VERY SMALL screw driver, or other small pointed object, gently insert it in the space (Fig. 8.) Working alternately from each side, spread the clasp connector just enough to remove it. In some extremely stubborn cases, very small needle nose pliers can be used. Do not try to hurry the removal.

Fig. 9

Once the clasp is off, replace it with the new one and ever so gently close the connector. Needle nose pliers are effective, taking care not to compress too hard or too fast. When it appears to be at the right point, try to close the clasp. It may be necessary to do this in several steps to avoid bending the clasp out of shape and rendering it useless. Again, practicing on throw-away pieces is suggested.

Replacing and repairing earring backs

Replacing glued-on earring backs is the simplest of repairs once the correct back is found. As with all repairs, clean the area to be repaired on both the piece and the replacement part. Refer to the intact earring for placement of the back and glue. If both backs are missing, or you are choosing to change the back, simply examine the pieces for indications of where the original backs were placed. We never recommend changing an original back as this greatly decreases the value, if not totally negating it.

In the case of clip-on earrings, should the back still be attached but the clamp be missing, there are two ways to go. One is to loosen the back by working around it with a sharp object, removing it, and replacing the entire back. The other option is to replace just the clamp. The design of the back determines the feasibility of this method. It is achieved by GENTLY spreading the two outside pieces holding the clamp (Fig. 9.), inserting the replacement piece, and tightening with needle nose pliers (Fig. 10.) This should be done with the clamp in the closed position. Several attempts may be needed to accomplish the desired results.

Fig. 10

Should the earring clamp be signed, it is best to try to locate a replacement with an identical signature. If the repair is being made simply to make them wearable, let your conscience be your guide.

Replacing pin backs

It is very difficult to replace an entire pin back (Fig. 11.) Soldering will sometimes work but, with the weight and pressure of wearing, it does not seem to hold for long. The glues currently on the market may also work for awhile. Your choice will depend greatly on the type of metal the piece is made of and the desired end result, and if it is for wear or display.

Fig. 11

Should the pin and clasp be individually attached (Fig. 12.), the chances of reattachment are minimal. Especially in the case of pieces made of pot metal, as the substance neither glues nor solders well. The drawback with glue is the amount needed to secure the back in place.

If the piece is one of your favorites, and you're willing to take the chance, we recommend locating someone who has had practice with soldering and give it a try. Usually one of your local antique stores will be willing to share them with you.

It is another story if just the pin itself is missing. In most cases this replacement is a simple process. First, refer to your collection of findings. The pin must be long enough to be secured in the clasp and yet not so long that it extends beyond the piece. If it is too long it will

Fig. 12

either be visible from the front or dangerous (the author recently lost just such a piece due to the pin extending too far, catching on something, and falling off unnoticed.)

Once the correct pin is located, the pin holder on the piece should be GENTLY spread apart (Fig. 13.) The circled end of the pin is then placed in the space, centering the circle in the center of the holder. Compress the holder with the needle nose pliers until the pin is secure and still able to rotate freely (Fig. 14.)

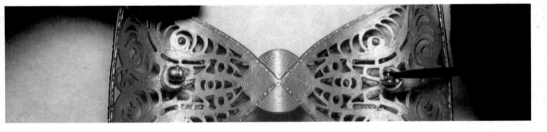

Fig. 13

Fig. 14

The replacement of the pin C-clasp is also fairly easy IF at least a part is still attached (Fig. 15.) Careful examination reveals two pieces are used. Depending on the piece, either the inside or outside of the C-clasp is moveable.

Fig. 15

The repair is much like that of the pin. Once again refer to the findings for an exact match.

In the case of the center piece rotating, spread the still attached part GENTLY (Fig. 16.) Insert the replacement part, center, and compress with the needle nose pliers (Fig. 17.), leaving just enough room for rotation.

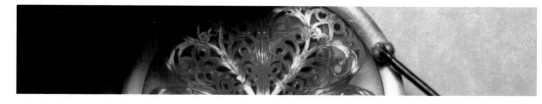

Fig. 16

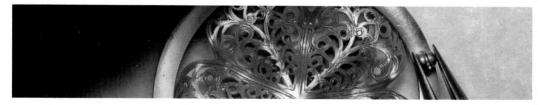

Fig. 17

When the outer portion is the rotating part, the repair is done in much the same manner (Fig. 18.) The difficult part is getting it secure enough to hold while still enabling some rotation. With nothing on either side to hold it, just the right amount of pressure is needed to make the repair effective. Trial and error are your best friends during this phase.

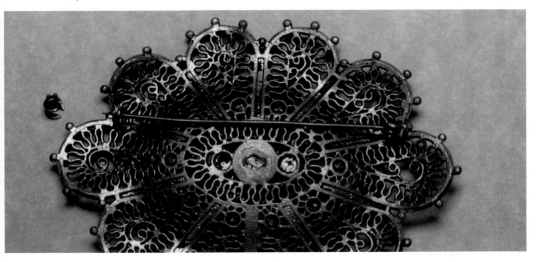

Fig. 18

When the exact match is found in your findings, place it over the attached "post." After centering same, compress with the needle nose pliers (Fig. 19.) until it is secure but still able to rotate.

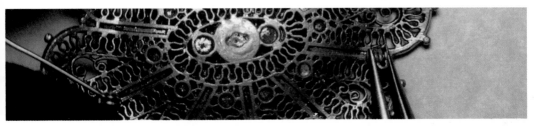

Fig. 19

There are two secrets to doing repairs yourself. First is practice, practice, practice. It is suggested that some throw-away pieces be experimented on so as not to ruin those that are treasured. Second is patience doing both the repair and locating the perfect match. In one case it took almost four years to find just the right stone to repair a beloved bracelet, but it was worth the wait. But don't give up, you can do it.

Chapter 3
Storage

How and where you choose to store your rhinestone treasures depends on the space available, your budget, and whether you plan to display them, wear them, or simply protect them. No matter which method you choose, there are three very important factors to consider.

First: temperature change. Any extreme change in temperature can affect stone settings and glues. Second: moisture. As we've discussed earlier, moisture is the worst enemy of costume jewelry. Not only can it destroy the foil backing of rhinestones, it can also cause great damage to the metals used. The green patina is familiar to us all and can irreversibly damage the most well-made piece. Third: space. Rhinestone jewelry must never be allowed to rest atop another piece or be jostled together. This can dislodge or scratch stones.

Displaying your collection can be as simple as a curio cabinet with the pieces arranged on the shelves in any way that pleases you. Should you choose to wear a treasure, they are readily available. Of course, if the collection is vast this may not be practical.

Another way we have observed is using shadow boxes and arranging them on a wall. Though this may be attractive, accessibility is a problem.

Antique dental cabinets are wonderful for storage. The many drawers are shallow and enable the collector to locate a given piece with very little effort. True, the collection is not on display, but very well protected. This is the choice of one of the authors.

There are shallow display cases available that can be lined and hold a good number of pieces. These can be slipped under a bed or chest ready for viewing or wearing at a moments notice.

Tried and true, individually wrapping and bagging each piece has its pros and cons. Although it is the most protective method, accessibility is time consuming and sometimes difficult.

The authors have also observed small collections on velvet covered cork board hung on a wall. We do not recommend this practice as dust and the elements can do great harm as well as put continual stress on the pins.

Again, we cannot stress enough the importance of protecting your collection. Time and money are involved in acquiring your pieces, treat them as an investment as well as a delight.

Chapter 4

Purple, Pink, and Red

Purple - "dark blend of red and blue"
Pink - "pale red color"
Red - "a primary color at the lower end of the spectrum"

From royalty to innocence.

The bracelet done in the Eisenberg style, is unsigned. It is obvious to even a novice collector that it is merely a copy cat piece. The earrings are also unsigned. Earrings $25-45. Bracelet $75-95.

Though unsigned, the design and depth of these stones create a very collectible piece. Necklace $60-85.

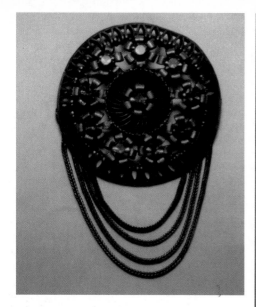

Scrolled metal work sets off the deep purple stones in this unique piece. Pin $75-105.

The combination of lavender rhinestones and opaque cabochons add interest to this set. Set $65-85.

Only the earrings of this lavender *Weiss* set are signed. Set $90-120.

Exploding unusual colors are typical of the *Regency* style. All pieces are signed. Set $100-125.

The pin is of marquise cut stones and can also be worn as a pendant. The amethyst necklace is of different size and shape prong set stones. Pin $45-60. Necklace $60-85.

Close up viewing reveals many unique stones and settings. Small purple stones are reverse set with points up in the Schreiner style. Light pink accent stones are actually clear and pink striped. No signature can be found on this piece which also converts to a pendant. Pin $80-120

Pave set rhinestones with faceted glass stones enhance this goldtone over sterling set. Set $100-125.

Only the earrings of this flowered set are signed *Weiss*. Set $70-95.

Palest of pinks are used in this *Eisenberg* signed bracelet. Bracelet $100-125.

These *CORO* signed pieces, although of the same design idea, are not a set but can be easily worn as such. Bracelet $35-50. Necklace $45-60.

Color and quality of the pink stones in all pieces are similar, even though by three different manufactures. Only the earrings are signed *Art* within a star and 1/20 12K GF. Earrings $45-60. Necklace $60-85. Pin $50-70.

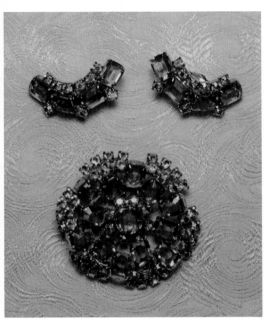

Pale pink rectangular stones are faceted colored glass and accent stones are aurora borealis. Set $65-85.

Pink, pink, and more pink. Fun to own and fun to wear. Round pin is marked Austria. Pins $35-60.

This 2.5" brooch is a must have although unsigned. Pin $45-65.

Pink cabochons are the focal point of all pieces. Only the pin with green accent stones is signed *Regency*. Pins $45-90. Earrings $25-45.

Clear rhinestones surround cabochons in this pair of dress clips. Clips $45-60.

Brilliant conical stones create this *Weiss* pin. Pin $55-75.

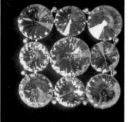

Pin is signed *Kramer of New York*. Bracelet is of lower quality and unsigned. Pin $45-60. Bracelet $35-50.

Pink rhinestone centers set off the enameled flowers in this *Sarah Coventry* pin and earring set. Set $55-75.

Reminiscent of the style used when setting precious stones and diamonds. Bracelet is marked Sterling, ring is signed *Hobe*, and dress clip is unsigned. Ring $75-100. Clip $40-65. Bracelet $100-125.

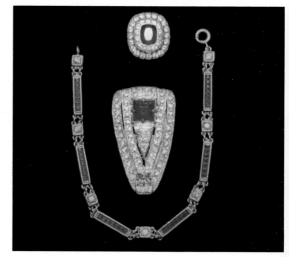

A combination of opaque and frosted stones are used in both bracelets. Bracelets $50-65.

Scalloped shaped necklace can be worn with pendant style earrings. Set $90-120.

Blood red stones are the central theme of these pieces. The necklace and bracelet are accentuated by the massive chain links, making this a very heavy set. The brooch is of faceted glass stones. Pin $65-95. Set $125-150.

Aurora borealis stones accent the red rhinestones in this 3" pin with matching earrings. Set $65-85.

The surrounding smoke colored stones make the red stones the center of attention in this piece. Pin $50-70.

Larger conical stones add a different dimension to this set. Set $50-70.

Both necklace and earrings are signed *Phyliss* 1/20 12K GF. Combination of stone shapes add to the design. Set $95-125.

Candy apple red color is used in a combination of foil backed and faceted glass stones. Pin $35-50. Bracelet $35-50. Set $45-60.

Earrings and pin of the same 2.5" length, sharing the idea of drops that move when worn. Earrings $45-65. Pin $60-85.

Snowflake pin can be converted to a pendant. All pins are examples of lower quality jewelry available at discount stores of the times. Pins $20-50.

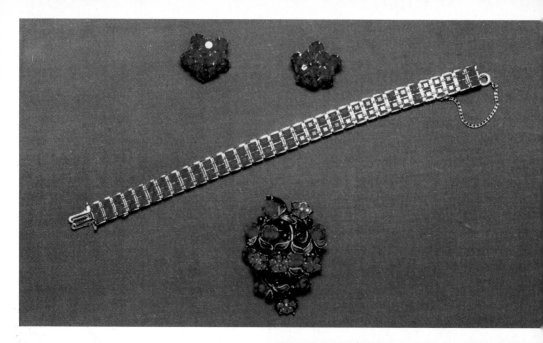

The pin demonstrates an interesting combination of stones, enameling, and japanning. Simple yet classy bracelet is one of several in various colors owned by the Authors. Earrings? No. Scatter pins purchased at a five and dime in the 1960s. Scatter pins $20-35. Pin $45-65. Bracelet $65-90.

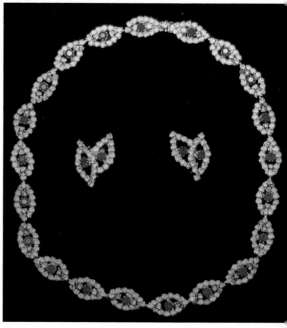

Though unmarked, the exceptional workmanship is evident in these pieces. Set $125-150.

One of the first pieces purchased by the Author. It is a contrast of rhinestones and rectangular opaques. Bracelet $65-85.

Chapter 5

Gold

Gold - "heavy yellow metallic"

Rhinestones set in gold metal allows each and everyone of us to feel the "Midas Touch."

Leaf earrings with open centers can be easily worn with the leaf bracelet. Note light and airy metalwork. Earrings $20-30. Bracelet $35-50.

Open center design with gold beading and foil backed rhinestones are used in this piece signed *Kramer.* Pin $65-90.

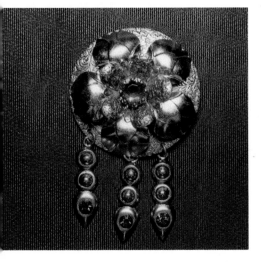

Dangling pendants add to an otherwise plain piece. Pin $50-75.

Slider bracelet utilizing different textures and stones as in victorian pieces it copies. Signed *Goldette N.Y. Bracelet $65-85.*

A combination of gold, blue rhinestones, pearls, and channel se clear rhinestones create this retro piece. Necklace $65-85.

The pin is one seen everywhere and signed *Coro*. The necklace achieves an interesting look by combining iridescent crystals, gold beads, and chains spaced with rhinestone rondelles. It is signed *Vendome*, the elite division of Coro. Pin $45-65. Necklace $165-185.

Delicate small pin convertible to pendant is signed *Scitarreli*. Pin $35-50.

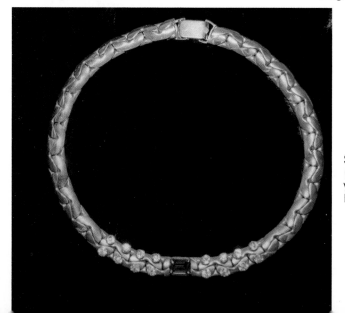

Single center emerald cut green stone makes this a simple yet elegant necklace. Necklace $65-90.

Lockets a pair. Bow and book signed *Coro* with original paper photos. Hearts and arrow features hand painted mother of pearl. Lockets $50-75.

Cuff bracelet of individual flowers, each with a colored rhinestone as the center. Bracelet $75-95.

Textured gold and rhinestones are used by all three designers. Left is signed *Lisner*, right is *J.J.*, and bottom is *B.S.K. Pins $45-65.*

Older *Trifari* fur clip employs different gold tone colors with pave set stones. Clip $135-160.

Pin and earrings for the bird lover, done in plated pot metal and paste set stones. They are unsigned. Set $75-100.

Left pin is of three gold tones with faceted glass center stone marked 1/20 12 k.g.f. with a capital I inside a capital H. Center pin is a combination of glass and foil backed stones signed *Coro Sterling Craft*. The pin on the right is simple and unsigned. Pins $20-55.

Paste set rhinestones and enameling accentuate this pin signed *Trifari*. Pin $65-85.

The pin on the left is signed *Taylord* 1/20 12k gold filled and is older than the unsigned pin on right. Pins $40-85.

Trifari signed bracelet with dainty pink flowers is one of 12 created for each month to simulate birthstones. Matching necklaces were also available. Bracelet $65-90.

This 3.5" pin is designed around the large 1" stone and simply marked silver Mexico. The bracelet is another marked 1/20 10k with a capital I inside a capital H. Pin $65-90. Bracelet $40-55.

The earrings have more rhinestones than immediately evident. They are signed *Hobe* both on the clips and the earrings themselves. The bracelet is unsigned and of a geometric design. Earrings $40-60. Bracelet $25-45.

Indicative of what was found at finer department stores across the country. Necklace $45-70.

Chapter 6
Yellow, Amber, and Brown

Yellow - "between red and green in the spectrum"
Amber - "brownish-yellow"
Brown - "combination of red, black, and yellow"

Warm autumn and earth tones are represented by these pieces.

Hobe set is just a little strange. What else can describe this combination of mottled opaque yellow glass and rhinestones? Both necklace and hinged cuff bracelet are signed. Set $175-250.

Another example of this decades styling. The only difference being pear shaped stones as opposed to marquises. Earrings $20-35. Pin $40-65.

Of this earring collection, only the pair on the right is signed *Coro*. A broad spectrum of yellows, browns, ambers, and oranges are displayed. Earrings $20-50.

Another combination of marquises using more aurora borealis stones in a flowing design. Set $60-85.

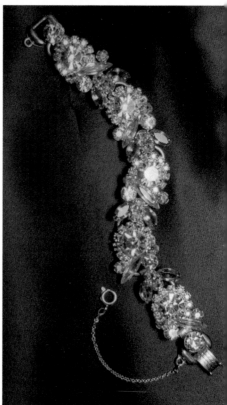

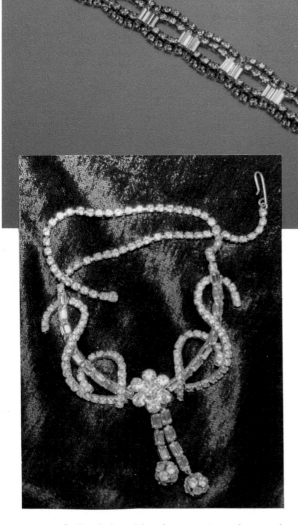

When bought the Author thought this bracelet was clear. Upon closer inspection one can see the pale yellow color of the stones. Bracelet $50-65.

Swirls of clear rhinestones over and around amber baguettes ending in rhinestone balls, creates this dramatic unsigned necklace. Necklace $80-100.

Each link uses a large center rhinestone of pale yellow surrounded by aurora borealis and transparent marquises. Bracelet $45-65.

This matched pair of scatter pins are signed *Simmons*. The delicate bracelet has three amber center accent stones. Pins $40-60. Bracelet $25-45.

Another of the popular clunky link bracelets with repeating design. Two inch drop earrings use square rhinestones set in the diamond shape. Earrings $25-40. Bracelet $45-65.

Simple but attractive designs which can easily be worn day or night. Earrings $20-35. Necklace $40-65.

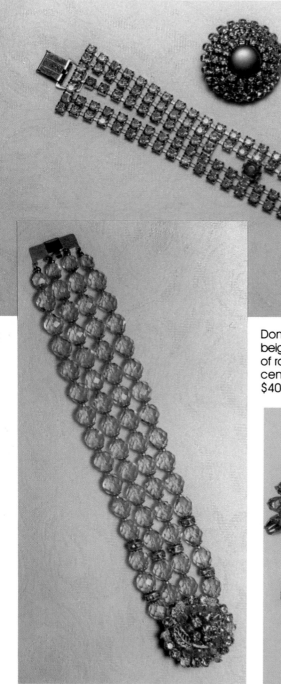

Domed earrings are 1.5" with pearlized beige center stone. The bracelet is five rows of round amber rhinestones with a darker center stone. Earrings $25-40. Bracelet $40-65.

Definitely *De Mario NY* as signed. Amber glass beads with amber rhinestones and rondelles. What a prize! Bracelet $200-225.

Marquise stones dominate all pieces, whether foil backed or transparent. An assortment of amber or aurora borealis stones are used for accent. All are unsigned in this grouping. Earrings $20-30. Pins $35-55.

The earrings are a smaller version of the matching pin in this unsigned set. Marquise cut stones are interspersed with aurora borealis. Set $60-85.

Wonderful design with enameled leaves accenting the large amber faceted glass stones. Small yellow rhinestones are evident if you look closely. Necklace $95-125.

An otherwise plain set is made interesting by the unique leaf stones with realistic veins and frosting on half the leaf. Set $50-75.

All pieces are signed *Regency* in this set of browns and golds. The authors recently saw the matching necklace and bracelet at an antique show, but were unable to locate the owner. Set $75-110.

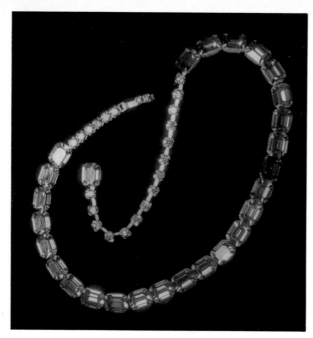

You would expect nothing less from *Weiss*. Exceptional quality stones are used in this necklace that has been seen in other colors as well. Necklace $75-100.

Maltese cross suspended from a mesh tab under a fleur de lis with open mouthed lions head. Signed *Florenza*, all stones are paste set. Pin $75-110.

Black metal sets off this brown and amber spray. The necklace of brown oval and emerald foiled stones is simple but classy. Pin $30-45. Necklace $40-55.

All pieces utilize larger than normal brown stones. The bracelet is primarily of pale yellow rhinestones. Earrings $25-45. Bracelet $30-50.

The pin signed *Hollycraft* is gold foiled rhinestones opening to a bud created by a gold over black glass stone. Daisy earrings are entirely of the same gold rhinestones. This type of stone was popular with other designers as evident in the next photos. Earrings $40-65. Pin $80-115.

Three very different designs are used in these two pins and earrings. Both earrings are signed *Weiss* and right pin is marked Made Austria. Earrings $35-50. Pins $35-65.

Yet another example of the gold rhine stones, this time silver and smoke have been incorporated. These berry shaped pieces are sadly unsigned. Set $95-130.

All but one earring are signed *Weiss* in this extraordinary set. The cuff bracelet is hinged in two places allowing for a better fit. A favorite of the author as it was a birthday gift from her husband. Set $185-215.

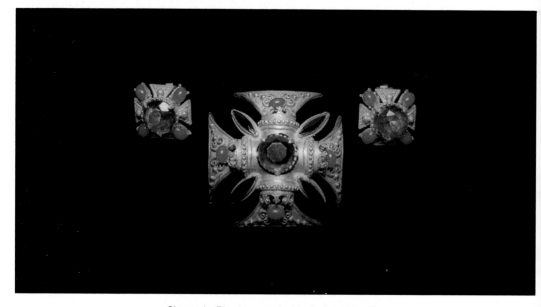

Signed *Florenza* on each piece, the maltese cross convertible pin and earrings are done in their usual baroque style. Set $85-125.

Chapter 7
Green

Green - "between blue and yellow in the spectrum"

A sign of new growth and spring.

Opaque cabochons with alternating
rhinestones are used in the 1" bracelet.
These pieces were once affordable to all.
Earrings $20-30. Bracelet $40-60.

Of the two pins, the spray is marked simply 7657 and is of better quality. Pins $45-75.

The crown and earrings are all signed *Weiss.* The stones are all flat foil backed. Set $125-150.

Seven large square stones hanging from a single strand of pale green rhinestones. Necklace $65-85.

Bracelet design similar to platinum pieces popular at the time. Upper pin is of green and smoke round rhinestones. Lower pin converts to pendant. Pins $25-50. Bracelet $115-135.

Two shades of green and two sizes of marquise stones have been used in this signed *Weiss* pin. Pin $55-75.

Carved glass stones resembling leaves and flowers. Only the necklace of this set is signed *Lisner*. Set $65-90.

Resembling a snail, this *Kramer* pin utilizes pave set rhinestones around a large opaque glass stone. Pin $75-105.

Signed *Schreiner New York*, the reverse mounted faceted stones along with the foil backed green stones exemplifies the Schreiner style. Pin $150-175.

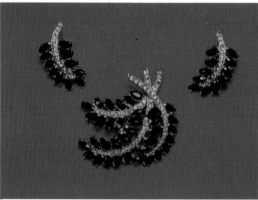

Minimal use of rhinestones in the center of enameling. Signed *HAR*, it is simpler than most of this designers work. Pin $75-100.

Wonderful rich *Hollycraft* set done with pave set clear and dark green oval stones. All pieces are signed. Set $95-125.

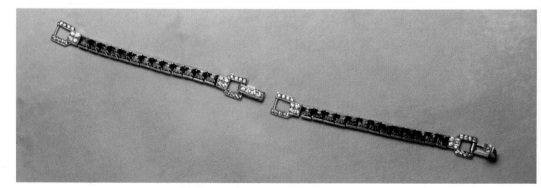

This truly unique bracelet can be opened and closed with either rhinestone clasp. Marked sterling on both clasps, it is of extraordinary workmanship. Bracelet $140-185.

The unknown designer was able to achieve a 3-D effect by overlaying clear rhinestones on the larger pear shaped stones. Necklace $100-125.

Unsigned bracelet of deep green stones with detailed metalwork. Bracelet $50-75.

Lots of shapes and a broad spectrum of color have been used in these unsigned pins. Pins $45-70.

This piece screamed "buy me," no matter the cost! Stones are large bright lime green. Bracelet $95-120.

The pin is defined by the light blue center stones. The earrings are signed *La Roco*. Earrings $35-55. Pin $50-65.

Dime store quality, but still fun and collectible due to green colors. Pins $35-50.

Faceted green stones between gold flowers with rhinestone centers creates a springtime piece. This bracelet is signed *Art*. Bracelet $110-125.

Typical *Weiss* quality stones are used in this signed bracelet. The pin, though complimentary, lacks the same depth. Pin $40-60. Bracelet $65-90.

The bracelet uses two sizes of cabochons with rhinestones. What a strange combination of stones showing design freedoms. Earrings $20-30. Bracelet $45-70.

Acquired at two different places, this is one of the authors' favorite sets. They are signed *Regency*. Set $140-185.

A swirl design with paste set stones create an attractive piece. Pin $50-75.

Fun combination of bigger earrings and slim double strand choker, both in dark green. Earrings $25-40. Necklace $50-65.

An array of celery green marquises and cabochons create this *Regency* pin. Pin $60-95.

Chapter 8
Blue

Blue - "between green and violet in the spectrum"

Blue skies, blue moon, deep blue seas, blue lagoon. This color conjures up feelings of calm and serenity.

Pin and earrings of transparent oddly shaped blue faceted stones using aurora borealis accents. Measures 2" across and 1" in depth. Set $75-100.

Aqua stones are all opaque or frosted marquise shaped. These pins show a different side of blue. Pins $50-75.

Three inch trefoil pin uses the same shade of blue throughout the design. Pin $55-75.

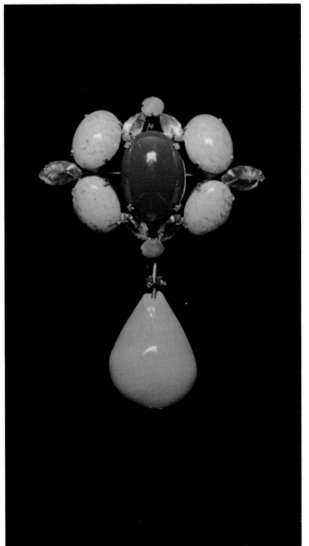

Scalloped stones are the centers of attraction in this magnificently well made necklace. Transparent marquise stones with blue and aurora borealis accents complete the design. The center piece is 4" long. Set $175-225.

Signed *Schreiner New York* and 3.5" from tip to tip, this brooch of cabochons is unusual. All accent stones are reverse set with facets up. No foiled stones are used in this piece. Pin $150-175.

Commanding 2" bracelet with unusual light blue domed cabochons. Bracelet $80-110.

Blazing blue foil backed stones illuminate this 3.5" pin. Pin $125-150.

Oval sapphire stones are set between round and baguette stones. The necklace clasp is stamped with a crown. Could this be Trifari? Set $85-110.

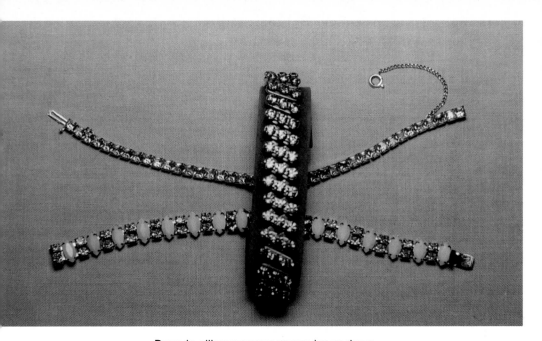

Done in either opaque marquise or deep set square stones, both clasp bracelets are signed *Weiss*. The expansion bracelet is desirable due to the color. Bracelets $45-85.

Bracelet and necklace, although unsigned, use quality stones showing excellent color. Either pair of earrings can be worn with this set. Earrings $20-40. Set $65-95.

All pieces have dark blue center stones surrounded by pale blue rhinestones. None are signed. Earrings $25-45. Bracelets $40-85.

Pot metal base with clear rhinestones and opaque cabochons. This pin measures 4" long and is unsigned. Pin $75-95.

The royalist of blues create a striking pairing of bracelet and earrings. Earrings $25-40. Bracelet $125-150.

The earrings use the same leaf motif as the clasp on the older brass necklace of brilliant bezel set stones. Earrings $30-50. Necklace $95-110.

A trio of chevrons. Upper and lower pins of pot metal and center a much older variety. Pins $35-60.

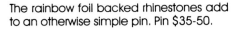

Joseph Wiesner N.Y. created this striking 3.5 " by 3" pin. Pin $150-175.

Minimal use of colored stones are shown in both pieces. Top pin has interestingly carved clear leaves. Pins $45-75.

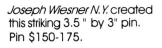

The rainbow foil backed rhinestones add to an otherwise simple pin. Pin $35-50.

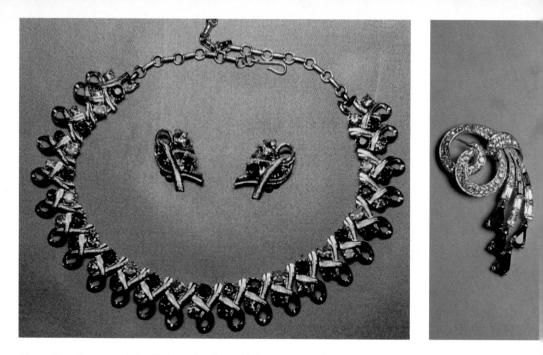

Silvertone metal with two shades of blue rhinestones and geometric design are used in this set signed *Coro*. Set $55-80.

Pave set rhinestones with dark blue pea shaped stones creates the beauty of *Boucher*. Pin $125-150.

Old and new meet in these three pieces. Gold filigree pin is marked Czechoslovakia. Paisley shaped pin is done in blue enameled metal. Pins $40-65. Earrings $25-40.

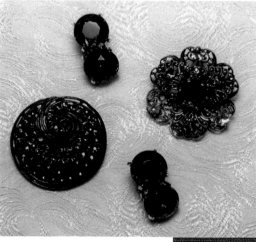

Each stone in this unsigned pin and earring set is a combination of transparent and opaque surrounded by blue rhinestones. Set $65-95.

Necklace of graduated stones is an ever popular design. Earrings feature large .5" stones. Earrings $35-55. Necklace $55-75.

Smokey blue cabochons create an unusual flowered bracelet. Bracelet $65-85.

Simple set indicative of the 1950s style, utilizing two very close shades of blue. Set $60-90.

The majority of stones in the *Weiss* signed pin are cabochons, as in the unsigned earrings. Earrings $25-35. Pin $75-95.

Paisley design with blues of several shades, all signed B.S.K. Set $55-75.

Feather shaped pin using royal blue faceted glass stones is 4.5" long. Pin $65-85.

Top earrings remind one of the Robert style, yet are unsigned. The bracelet is of a heavy metal enhanced by blue cabochons. Bottom earrings are also quite heavy, but with excellent stones. Earrings $35-50. Bracelet $45-60.

Diverse assortment of fun to wear earrings. Earrings $20-50.

Silver scroll overlays bring out the royal blue color in all stones used in this set. Set $85-110.

Many different colors and types of stones are used in these two pins. Top piece is marked Austria. Pins $45-75.

Each link repeats with a large pink cabochon, two molded marquises, and a single blue rhinestone. The earrings use the same pattern. Set $50-75.

Seldom do earrings and pin match so well. Although unsigned, these are a treasure to own. A bracelet to this set does exist as we have seen in another publication. Set $100-135.

All pieces are *Coro*, though the necklace is unsigned. Earrings $25-40. Set $60-85.

Signed *Hollycraft Corp. 1956*, this necklac
exemplifies the makers' trademark styl‹
using various shades of the same col‹
stones that are all paste set. Necklac
$150-175.

Opaque cabochons add to the beau
of each of these pieces. Pin $25-45. Nec
lace $50-75.

The bracelet is signed *KTF* denoting Trifari,
Kraussman, Fishel, Inc. Bracelet $95-115.

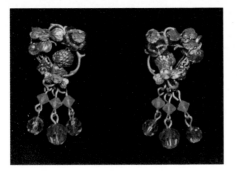

These earrings are signed *Eugene* and are composed of colored crystal beads and rhinestones. Earrings $85-110.

From the delicate silver chain to the detailed metal work, this necklace uses blue and silver rhinestones to accomplish the appealing end result. Necklace $65-90.

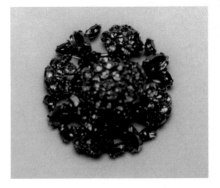

Although reminiscent of the Schreiner style, this brooch is unsigned. Quality and color of stones is remarkable. Pin $100-125.

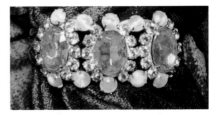

This almost luminescent periwinkle blue set stamped Made in Austria on an applied oval is another of the authors' favorites. The depth of the stones is incredible and difficult to capture on film. Set $100-125.

Hinged cuff bracelet with 1" center stones, small opaque cabochons, and aurora borealis stones is a real attention getter. Bracelet $90-110.

Signed *Eisenberg Ice*, this pin and brace-let have been seen in clear, pinks, purples, and golds. This clearly demonstrates not only a popular design but quality stones used consistently by the manufacturer. Pin $125-150. Bracelet $150-175.

Three earrings? No, a pair of earrings and a cocktail ring all signed *Judy Lee*. Note the unusual center cabochons. Set $60-85.

Individual pieces yet both use large ba guettes and round rhinestones. The brace let is signed *Weiss*. Pin $35-50. Bracele $60-85.

Vibrant turquoise color dominates this pic ture. Conical shaped stones are used in the circular *Weiss* pin on the right. Though lei pin looks to be crystal, it is actually of re verse aurora borealis. Pins $45-75.

Close scrutiny reveals many unique stones from faux Venetian glass to large pink/blue faceted stones to center cabochon of glass molded with metal flakes. Pins $45-70.

Pins are similar design using marquise stones. Pins $40-55.

The transparency of this pin picks up whatever color it is worn on. The large stones are two toned green and blue. Set $75-100.

Bracelet is signed *Weiss* and has been seen in other colors using aurora borealis spacers. Earrings have an unusual carved marbled accent stone. Earrings $20-35. Bracelet $65-85.

Each piece of this grouping uses pale blue round rhinestones that are prong set. Only the bracelet is signed *Weiss*. Pins $15-55. Bracelet $50-75. Necklace $35-55.

Small pin is marked Made in Germany, while others are unsigned. Large pin is of oval, emerald, and round stones. The earrings use aurora borealis for added color. Earrings $20-30. Pins $25-65.

Expansion bracelet is unusual because of the aqua colored stones down the center. It is marked Made in U.S.A. The earrings are early 1950s and look great with the bracelet. Earrings $30-50. Bracelet $50-70.

Vibrant periwinkle blue rhinestone with three large drops becomes a 1.75" pin signed *Weiss*. Pin $60-95.

Chapter 9

Aurora Borealis

Aurora Borealis - "luminous streamers of light; northern lights"

The epitome of the word "Rainbow." Every possible color imaginable lends its hues to this chapter.

The three inch hanging array of stones immediately draws one's attention. All pieces consist of small brown rhinestones and aurora borealis centered by large faceted transparent stones. This set is unsigned. Set $125-150.

The bracelet of frosted marquises and cabochons is framed by the identical green aurora borealis stones used in the necklace. Bracelet $30-50. Necklace $35-50.

The unsigned bracelet certainly looks nice with the *Weiss* signed swirl pin. The greens and blue/green aurora borealis are dead ringers. Pin $50-75. Bracelet $35-50.

Colors to fool the eye. All round stones are pink/red aurora borealis with remaining baguettes of topaz. Wonderful design with unusual twists and turns. Set $85-110.

The deep blue/purple aurora borealis stones are such a contrast to the clear round rhinestones. Set $85-100.

Set in gold metal, the shades of blues and greens are accentuated by aurora borealis stones. Set $65-85.

Gauntlet style bracelet (open at the back with no hinge) and pin of pink and pink aurora borealis stones are both unsigned. Pin $35-50. Bracelet $35-50.

This unsigned 3" star or starfish is very well made. Each aurora borealis stone is prong set. Pin $90-110.

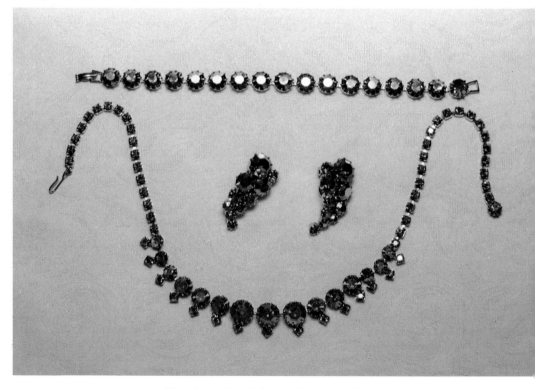

All unsigned and done of blue/purple aurora borealis in all sizes of round prong set stones. Earrings $25-40. Bracelet $30-50. Necklace $40-65.

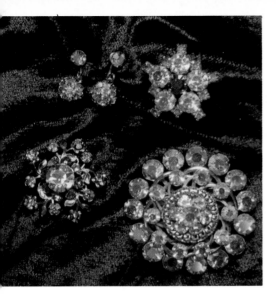

All pieces are prong set. The ball drop earrings are signed *Weiss*; upper right pin is marked Made in Germany. Earrings $30-45. Pins $25-55.

Pin and earrings with brown foil backed marquises and orange/pink aurora borealis appear to match, but are just a little different. A prime example of how companies used the same design. Earrings $25-35. Pin $35-55.

Three different shades of blue aurora borealis are arranged in these pieces. The center pin is 2.5" wide. The pin on the top is the only one to utilize clear rhinestones. The earrings are signed *Weiss*. Earrings $35-55. Pins $35-60.

Done completely in round blue/pink aurora borealis, these two necklaces reflect the endless styles produced. Necklaces $35-65.

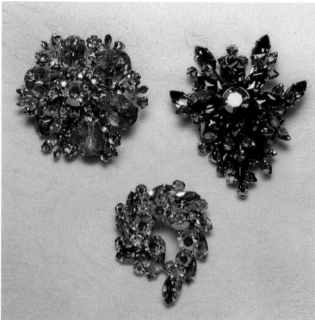

The pin on the left is of .75" foil backed rhinestones interspersed with aurora borealis stones. The right pin is of dark blue marquises, aurora borealis, and three iridescent molded glass stones. Last, but certainly not least, the bottom pin is signed *Weiss* and is of lavender marquise and aurora borealis stones. Pins $40-85.

The top bracelet is of lavender rhinestones centered with aurora borealis. The bottom bracelet is entirely of aurora borealis stones. Both are of the same era and are unsigned. Bracelets $35-55.

Weiss did both of these pieces in aurora borealis. The bracelet is a bit lighter, while the necklace exudes color. Bracelet $55-75. Necklace $75-100.

Weiss bracelet and unsigned pin look great when worn with denim. Circle pin has a definite top and bottom due to graduated stones. Pin $30-45. Bracelet $55-75.

This is another unmistakable set found in two separate locations. Light and airy gold design with aurora borealis accents. Set $45-70.

All unsigned and using different quality aurora borealis, the upper pin has square cut stones. Pins $25-45. Bracelet $30-50.

The silver bracelet is 1.5" wide with a single row of blue/green aurora borealis and is signed *Coro*. The earrings use a deeper shade of the same color set in gold. Earrings $25-35. Bracelet $40-60.

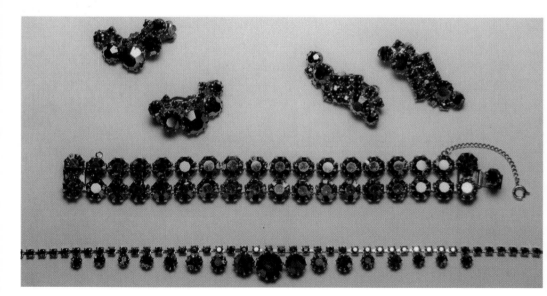

Every single stone in this photograph is a round blue/green aurora borealis. None of the pieces are signed. Earrings $30-45. Bracelet $50-65. Necklace $40-55.

Extraordinary *Weiss* set focusing on marquise aurora borealis surrounded by clear rhinestones. The bracelet is unique in the fact that all pieces are moveable on the two strand silver base in the slider fashion. Set $125-175.

Signed *Joseph Mazer*, this exceptional bracelet is of large emerald cut aurora borealis alternating with large "moonstones" and separated by three-stone rows. Bracelet $160-195.

Frosted stones run down the center of each bracelet and are framed in aurora borealis stones. Bracelets $25-50.

Unusual colors create this *Weiss* signed necklace and bracelet done primarily in shades of gold and tan rhinestones with a few peach aurora borealis accents. Set $100-125.

The circle pin combines large red and red aurora borealis stones divided by a line of four prong set red rhinestones. The earrings begin with the same aurora borealis and drop to red crystals and aurora borealis beads. Earrings $35-50. Pin $35-50.

The open circle pin of pink rhinestones and pink aurora borealis is signed *Karu Arke Inc.* The complimentary bracelet is entirely of pink aurora borealis. Pin $45-65. Bracelet $30-45.

Blues and greens delicately flow in these pins marked Made in Austria. The bracelet uses some of the same colors, but was made much later. Pins $35-50. Bracelet $30-45.

Deep turquoise aurora borealis stones make these lower end pieces appear of better quality than they actually are. Earrings $25-40. Pin $35-60. Bracelet $35-45.

Of these four pieces, only the top right pin is signed *Lisner*. This shade of blue aurora borealis was extremely popular in the late 1950s and early 1960s. Pins $25-50. Bracelet $30-50.

Simple statement in red/purple aurora borealis with each round stone prong set. Bracelet $35-55. Necklace $40-60.

Regency used the same basic design in these pins. One uses pink and fuchsia rhinestones with pink aurora borealis accents. The other, more reds with interestingly carved aurora borealis leaves. Pins $60-90.

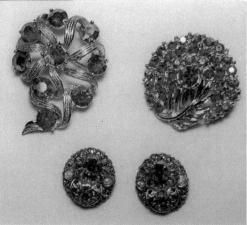

Trio of signed *Weiss* pins sharing diversity of green aurora borealis stones and incorporating many facets. Note attached green crystal dangling beads on the left pin. Pins $55-90.

Red/purple aurora borealis throughout these gold mountings adds sparkle and color. The left pin is signed *Kramer* and the earrings are marked West Germany. Earrings $20-30. Pins $35-60.

This group of pins all utilize the same shade of blue/green aurora borealis stones. The pin on the right is signed *Coro* and is paste set as opposed to the prong setting used in the other two. Pins $35-50.

Single strand aurora borealis bracelet was done in many other colors. The pin is a graceful design of gold, teardrop shaped pearls, and aurora borealis. Pin $35-50. Bracelet $35-50.

Though not easily found, both authors have identical bracelets in this color. All pieces use shades of green and aurora borealis. The pin is signed *Karu Arke Inc.* Earrings $25-35. Pin $45-65. Bracelets $30-45.

Three piece set entirely of pink and blue aurora borealis stones. None are signed. Set $85-105.

Crescent shaped 3" pin using pearls, green rhinestones, and aurora borealis. Scatter pins are signed *AJC*. Pin $55-85. Scatter pins $25-35.

Marquises of olive green and green aurora borealis dominate this *Regency Jewels* pin alongside its twin done in pinks and signed the same. Pins $60-90.

Red aurora borealis stones set in interlocking gold leaf shapes make up this three piece unsigned set. Set $65-95.

Clunky link bracelet with repeating use of pearls, aurora borealis, and blue aurora borealis with matching earrings. Set $50-75.

Large 1" black oval opaque stones surrounded by aurora borealis meet at the center of this hinged cuff bracelet. Bracelet $95-110.

Utilizing either rhinestones or aurora borealis in pink, these three individual pieces are unsigned and constitute a lovely grouping. Earrings $25-35. Pin $45-65. Bracelet $30-50.

This bracelet is signed *Hollycraft Corp. 1956* on each end link. All round stones are aurora borealis with turquoise aurora borealis marquises. Each stone is paste set, typical of their work. Bracelet $65-95.

Weiss again creates an interesting combination of colors in this open center pin. Pin $55-75.

Bracelet and brooch were not bought as a set. Both use foil glass cabochons, red rhinestones, and red/pink aurora borealis. Pin $65-95. Bracelet $70-100.

Done in a pillow style, the blue/green aurora borealis stones are all paste set in black metal. This set is unsigned. Set $75-105.

Earrings and 4" pin are all signed *Weiss*. Round and marquise cut stones are either celery green rhinestones or aurora borealis. Set $95-125.

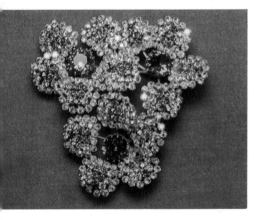

The outstanding lower pair of earrings are marked Austria and have unbelievable depth and color! The other pairs, though nice, can't compare. Earrings $30-65.

Fifteen small "flowers" create three larger flowers, all with deep purple centers. Aurora borealis stones seem to take on that same purple tint. Pin $125-150.

What a strange cut! These aurora borealis stones are flat on the top and carved at the sides. Pin $40-60.

In a kaleidoscope of colors, this *Weiss* signed double hinged bracelet runs the gambit of stone shapes and sizes. What a beauty! Bracelet $125-160.

Chapter 10

Multi-Colored

Multi - "consisting of many colors"

Any color combination you can imagine and some you can't are combined to create wonderful jewelry.

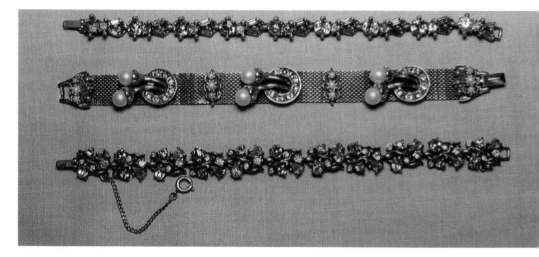

Three bracelets all with a variety of colors and shapes that are all paste set. Top bracelet is signed *Hollycraft Corp. 1955* and bottom is *Hollycraft Corp. 1950*. The center example is unsigned. Bracelets $45-95.

Nothing spectacular here, but sets we've all seen and bought in the beginning of our collections. Earrings $20-30. Set $25-45.

All pieces are signed *Sarah Coventry.* Mottled teardrop glass cabochons with paste set aurora borealis and faux pearls are used in this home sold set. Set $55-65.

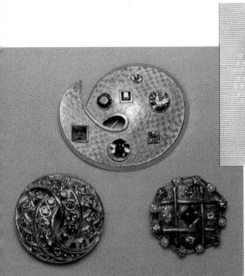

Iridescent scalloped edge stones appear to change colors with movement in their clustered setting. Pin centers are small aurora borealis stones. Earrings $25-45. Pin $65-85.

Three gold pins with minimal use of color. Pin on the left is signed *Hobe*. Pins $25-55.

Repetitive design of large pink cabochons, pink rhinestones, and green marquise cabochons give this unsigned set a distinctive flair. Set $65-85.

Look closely at the teardrop shaped stones. Not only are they foil backed faceted glass, but they are also variegated in color. This set is signed *Kramer*. Set $95-115.

What a center stone! Of this 3" pin, 1" alone is the center rainbow stone. From there, accent marquises and round red and aurora borealis stones create a starburst effect. Pin $65-85.

Right pin is of transparent faceted marquise stones, creating a leaf effect with a row of pink foil back center stones. Signed *B.S.K.*, the left pin again uses the transparent stones with rhinestone accents even to the ends. Pins $40-65.

Lacy metalwork with rhinestone flowers and sprigs using small turquoise round stones for accents. The pin is signed *B.S.K.* Set $50-75.

Signed *Weiss*, the large pink stones are faceted on both top and bottom and set off by deep blue marquises. Note the odd use of a rose pink pearlized stone. Pin $65-85.

Rust, greens, and oranges layered for an almost 3-D effect. Pin $40-55.

Only the green rhinestones are foiled on this unique pin with three pendulums. The cabochons have a pinkish purple jellied appearance. Pin $90-115.

Green and pink rhinestones accent flowers with pearl centers in this set signed *Coro*. Set $50-75.

Unique older bracelet signed *Selini* which incorporates pearls, green cabochons, and deep purple rhinestones. The necklace of the same vintage features a large pink glass cabochon. These two pieces definitely compliment each other. Bracelet $95-110. Necklace $50-85.

Large stones of all pieces appear to have metallic confetti floating in a sea of color. Earring $20-35. Pin $40-65.

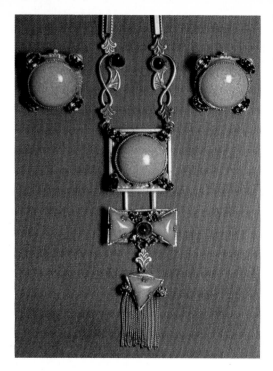

Each and every stone in this pair of earrings is a rainbow rhinestone with pink, blue, and green running through clear. The center stone of the pin is a larger version of the same stone accented by pink and red rhinestones surrounded by red teardrop cabochons. Earrings $35-50. Pin $35-50.

Excellent workmanship marked simply Germany on the clasp. This unusual necklace and earring set combines larger green stones accented by foiled amethyst marquises and domed cabochons. Set $150-200.

All stones in this 2.5" by 2" pin are foil backed, using eight different cuts in various sizes and colors. Pin $55-75.

Absolutely spectacular hinged bracelet! The .75" center conical stone is surrounded by a multitude of colors and shapes. Bracelet $150-175.

Shades of blue and green stones with an assortment of different cuts are used in these three pins which span many years. Top right pin is signed *Kramer*. Pins $25-90.

Imposing three piece set with yellow/green stones separated by curved blue cabochons. All pieces are signed *Florenza* in many places. The bracelet on each end, each earring, and the necklace on each link. Set $175-225.

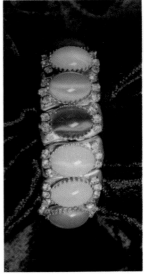

Olive green and brown elongated marquise stones are used in all pieces. The pin on the right is a symmetrical 2.5" starburst. Pin $50-70. Set $65-95.

Almost 1" glass cabochons in seven pastel colors with rhinestones at each end accentuate the fact that this is a very large expansion bracelet. Bracelet $55-75.

These unsigned pieces sparkle with the strange combination of pink, purple, and orange. Earrings $25-45. Bracelet $40-60.

Entirely of transparent glass marquises, save for the aurora borealis accent stones, this set tends to take on any color it is worn with. Set $55-75.

Delicate unsigned pin, once more utilizing many various cuts and colors. The two carved watermelon colored stones at the top are the only unfoiled stones used. The top bar is stationary while the remainder is free to move. Pin $85-110.

A 4" spray of deep purple pear shaped rhinestones with iridescent transparent cabochons. Pin $50-75.

Definitely Austria as marked, these stones have a depth and glitter all their own in smoke and gold. Set $65-85.

Crest like pin done in minute cabochons with pearls. Bracelet of enameling, rhinestones, and cabochons. Both are signed *Art*. Pin $65-95. Bracelet $50-75.

Dress clip on the left is of gold and lavender rhinestones. The spray is of simulated baroque pearls surrounded by pink rhinestones with multicolored cabochons. Clip $40-60. Pin $40-65.

Central to all pieces are the faux opal cabochons. The pin on the left is signed *Florenza*. The set consisting of pin and earrings is signed *Sphinx* and A510. The right pin is signed *Art*. Pins $45-75. Set $60-90.

One inch wide and using green, blue, and purple stones accented by blue cabochons, this bracelet creates a striking accessory. Bracelet $65-90.

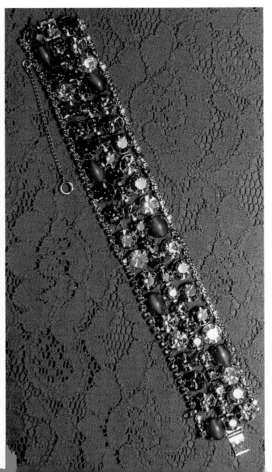

Signed *Coro* on the necklace and both earrings, this set relies on unique colored stones and few accent rhinestones. Set $65-85.

The top earrings are both signed *Weiss*. The bottom earrings and pin are an unsigned set. The combination of exceptional pastel rhinestones is dazzling. Earrings $45-65. Set $70-110.

Chapter 11
Black, Smoke, and White

Black - "darkest color; totally without light"
Smoke - "declouding and obscuring"
White - "radiated, transmitted, or reflected light containing all the rays of the spectrum"

From the black of night to the white of day, only the smokey time of dusk separates the two.

This 4" pin and earrings combines black opaque marquises with aurora borealis stones. Set $75-95.

Black on black best describes these pins. Open center pin is signed *Weiss*. Pins $40-85.

A sprinkling of clear and aurora borealis stones throughout these black pieces set in gold. None are signed. Earrings $20-30. Pin $30-50. Bracelet $25-40.

Five strand necklace with matching earrings features frosted glass beads with polished circles and rhinestone ball spacers. Set $110-140.

Black, brass, and rhinestone trefoil signed *Karu Arke Inc.* Pin $75-100.

Although using only clear rhinestones, these pieces appear black due to the japanned metal. Pins $30-75.

Bracelet and earrings combine clear rhinestones and black marquise cabochons. Pin also uses rhinestones but with black pear cut stones. Earrings $20-30. Pin $25-40. Bracelet $35-55.

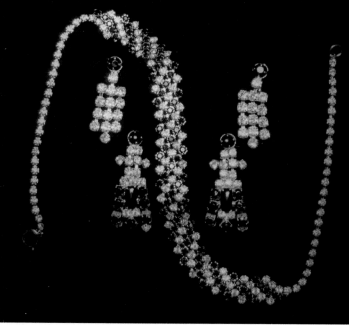

Dangle earrings, popular in the 1950s, accompanied by a geometric design necklace of alternating rows of black and clear rhinestones. Earrings $30-45. Necklace $50-70.

Smokey silver flat backed rhinestones are used in the leaf pin which is signed *Weiss* (in raised letters.) The bracelet consists entirely of baguettes except for the two round rhinestones on the clasp. Pin $85-100. Bracelet $70-95.

Transparent and foil backed stones are nicely arranged in this necklace and earring set. Set $75-110.

Spray pin is marked Made in Austria. The bracelet is 1" wide and includes black emerald cut stones. The earrings are simple black faceted stones surrounded by channel set rhinestones. Earrings $20-35. Pin $35-50. Bracelet $45-60.

The earrings and pin are signed *Cathe*, while the bracelet is unsigned. One must look closely to tell that they are not truly a set. Bracelet $55-75. Set $85-110.

Extremely large black teardrop stones are used to the utmost advantage in this three piece unsigned set. Set $150-175.

Marked Made in West Germany, this set combines gold filigree, pearls, and smokey silver cabochons. Set $60-80.

Smoke cabochons, amber rhinestones, and aurora borealis stones are lumped together in this asymmetrical pin with earrings. Set $75-95.

Upper earrings are faceted transparent glass, while the lower pair are foil backed. The pin is of glass cabochons with aurora borealis centers. Earrings $20-35. Pin $35-50.

Left pin is of large smoke glass cabochons with a rose carved center stone. Center pin is 6" long with 1" center stone and signed *Goldette*. Right pin has an exceptional smokey grey center stone. Pins $45-75.

This set is done entirely of smoke rhinestones. Baguettes line the loops of the necklace. Set $65-85.

Smaller bracelet utilizes cabochons and iridescent carved leaf stones in japanned metal. The larger bracelet relies on opaque white cabochons and faceted black stones for its motif. Bracelets $45-65.

Black and white on gold metal creates a springtime look. Necklace and earrings are a set. Pin $35-50. Set $45-60.

Dramatic spiral wrap bracelet of white and black glass beads. The rhinestone rondelles truly add to the design as well as the baguettes used at the head of each droplet. Bracelet $75-95.

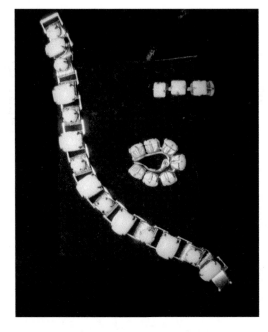

Along the same lines, these two separate designs wear well together. Earrings $20-35. Bracelet $25-45.

Necklace of round cabochons with two accent sizes in the drop. Bracelet is entirely of marquise shaped cabochons. Bracelet $35-50. Necklace $35-50.

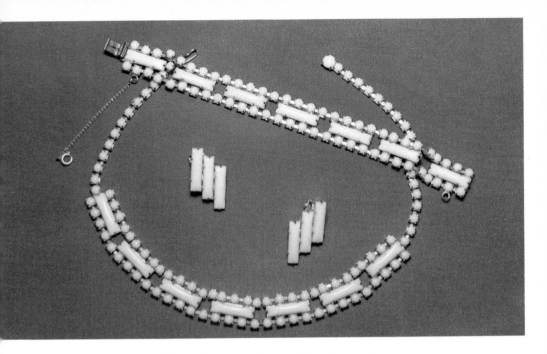

Milky white cabochon set looks great
against a healthy summer glow. Set $75-
90.

All with the ever popular white cabochons,
these three bracelets range from the delicate to dramatic. Bottom bracelet is signed
Trifari. Bracelets $30-60.

Both swirl pins are done in white cabochons set in gold metal. One uses clear rhinestones for accent while the other uses aurora borealis. Pins $35-65.

White and clear always create such a clean look. The two top pins use cabochons. The bottom pin is of faceted opaque glass marquises and signed *Weiss*. Pins $30-75.

This set employs elongated cabochons attached to a single row of rhinestones. Set $50-75.

A myriad of white cabochons and clear rhinestones are displayed in this 1940s to 1960s earring collection. Earrings $25-45.

Patriotism reigns with these two pieces. Bottom pin is signed *Weiss* in the raised letter format. Pins $30-75.

Entirely of cabochons, this set has that southwestern flair so popular today. Set $50-70.

Chapter 12
Pearl

Pearl - "usually white or blueish gray"

You don't need pearl divers to bring these beauties up from the seas.

Gold and pearls in assorted dimensions with rhinestones as sparkling accents. The bracelets remind one of several designers but are both unsigned. Pin $35-55. Bracelets $75-95.

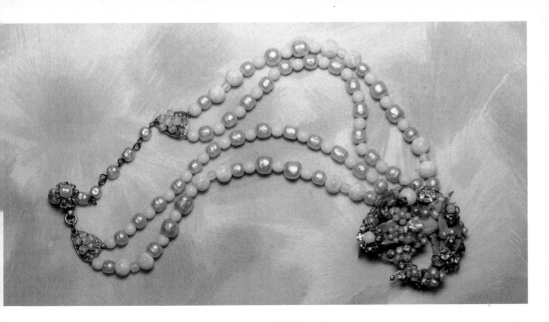

The necklace uses pearls, rhinestones, and glass beads in this wonderful style. The flowered hook is signed *Miriam Haskell*. Necklace $125-175.

Individual rhinestone clasps set each of these pearl bracelets apart from the other. The center bracelet is signed *Trifari* on the sterling stamped clasp. Bracelets $35-95.

Of pearl and rhinestone rondelles, the author remembers her mother wearing this set on special occasions. The necklace clasp is signed with an H inside a diamond. Set $65-95.

Same earrings in different sizes feature channel set rhinestones around pearl centers. The pin is delicately done in the same mediums. Earrings $20-35. Pin $25-45.

Trifari created this peas in a pod whimsy with an elegant touch. Pin $60-95.

Crescent shaped colored rhinestone clasp makes this pearl bracelet. Bracelet $30-50.

Talk about your dime store copies of the great designers. Choker and earrings are done in three colors of faux pearls with very few rhinestones. Set $40-60.

Five strands of gold chains and pearls come together at the 1" amethyst center stone and the .5" clasp stone. Bracelet $40-65.

Pin is an unusual combination of gold rhinestone marquises and pearls. The earrings practically cover the ear and are signed *Wirth of California*. Earrings $50-70. Pin $35-50.

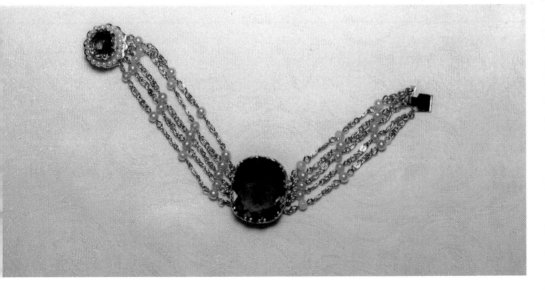

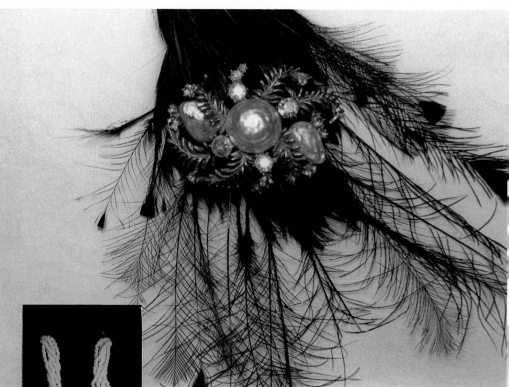

We know this *Har* signed pin has a matching bracelet. The baroque pearl stones
overpower this piece. Pin $85-110.

In the original box, this necklace can either be worn with the rhinestone and pearl
center to the back or front depending on
your daring. Necklace $50-75.

Chapter 13

Clear and Frosted

Clear - "bright, light, without color"
Frosted - "crystalline coating; covered or whitened with frost"

Clean and elegant, the icy touch of crystal clear stones enhances any look one strives to create.

Three different sizes of round rhinestones are used in this bold set. The *Kramer* signature is on the earring itself and on the necklace hook. Set $175-200.

Quality *Trifari* set of interlocking gold ovals and rhinestones. All pieces are signed. Set $80-100.

Exceptional, elegant, and ethereal defines this 3.5" of workmanship. Pin $90-110.

Choker and bracelet are simple, under-stated, and unsigned. Set $55-70.

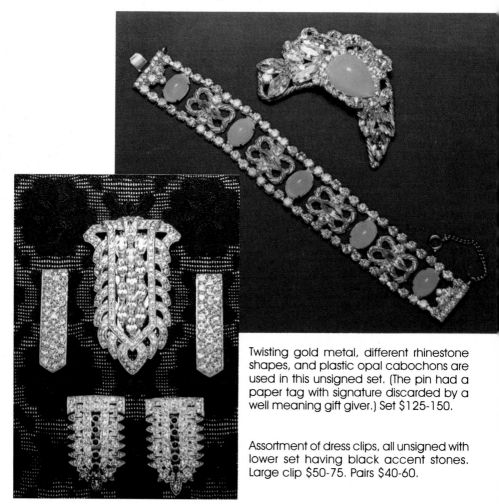

Twisting gold metal, different rhinestone shapes, and plastic opal cabochons are used in this unsigned set. (The pin had a paper tag with signature discarded by a well meaning gift giver.) Set $125-150.

Assortment of dress clips, all unsigned with lower set having black accent stones. Large clip $50-75. Pairs $40-60.

Two spray pins in eye catching designs utilizing various stones and placements. The right piece is signed *Coro* with a patent number. Pins $50-95.

Red cabochons accent this pin which uses the leaf motif in both overall shape and individual carved stones. Pin $110-135.

Representative of many reasonably priced sets our mothers received yearly. Set $45-65.

Measuring 5" long and truly an attention getter with the swaying pearl. Pin $90-110.

Different pieces, same idea and use of
stones. Bracelet $25-40. Necklaces $40-
55.

Note the similarity in design between these
unsigned pieces and the following Kramer
pieces. Pin $50-70. Necklace $50-75.

Kramer bracelet and *Kramer of N Y* necklace are of different decades but retaining same basic design. Bracelet $85-100. Necklace $95-120.

Bold, beautiful, and brilliant. All appropriate adjectives for this 4" unsigned piece. Pin $90-110.

Eisenberg has come a long way baby! This fur clip signed *Eisenberg Original* is one of the earlier pieces. Only the center stone remotely compares to their later quality. Clip $175-200.

Definitely trying to copy the famous Eisenberg style, including top overlay scrolls. Bracelet $75-95.

Located between the bracelets, the earrings are marked Austria. It is hard to tell them from the remaining scatter pins. Earrings $20-30. Pins $10-20. Bracelets $30-50.

Clunky link necklace signed *B & W* using three sizes of round glued in stones. Necklace $85-100.

Wonderful example of why unsigned jewelry is collectible. Pin $70-95.

Collection of expansion bracelets. Three nd four rows of rhinestones of different quality and settings. One is signed *Crite-on* and another *Lady Patricia made in Occupied Japan*. Bracelets $30-90.

Eisenberg Ice pin accented by dangling marquise cut stone. Pin $125-150.

Round, marquise, and bagette stones are used to enhance each of these unsigned bracelets. Bracelets $55-110.

Heavenly moons, stars, and a comet against the blue sky. Crescent shaped earrings, star scatter pins and comet anchored at either end. Earrings $25-40. Pins $15-60.

Flowery, fabulous, and fake aptly describes this large 3" pin. Pin $90-110.

Cascading waterfall necklace by *Hober* and earrings by *Weiss* look to be made for each other. Earrings $60-75. Necklace $165-190.

Note metal accents on pin which can be worn well with bracelet marked Austria. Pin $30-50. Bracelet $40-60.

Though the bracelet is unsigned, it is a perfect match for the *Weiss* pin. The necklace is of exceptional craftsmanship. Pin $65-90. Bracelet $40-55. Necklace $75-90.

Both pieces incorporate round prong set rhinestones. The bracelet is 1.5" wide. Pin $35-45. Bracelet $50-65.

The unsigned pin is remarkably similar to the *Kramer of N.Y.* bracelet. Pin $45-65. Bracelet $95-110.

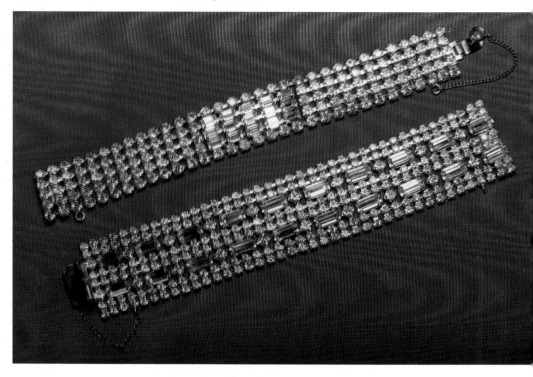

Stunning bracelets of excellent quality. Note additional bagettes on clasp of the larger 1.5" example. Bracelets $65-95.

Dynamic, dazzling, and dramatic. A combination of stone shapes and sizes are used on this 2.5" piece. Pin $90-110.

Although signed *Eisenberg Ice*, this is one of the Authors' least favorite pins. Pin $125-150.

Bracelet of uniform deeply prong set stones. Earrings are signed *Kramer*. Earrings $40-60. Bracelet $50-65.

Hinged cuff bracelet sparkles with every movement. Rhinestones only on the upper side. Bracelet $90-110.

This bracelet is identical to one in red seen previously in this book. Pins $30-45. Bracelet $50-75.

Lace background sets off delicate snowflake shaped pins. Pins $15-45.

Large emerald cut stones draw the eye to the center of each piece. Larger pin is signed *Coro*. Pins $15-50. Bracelet $50-65.

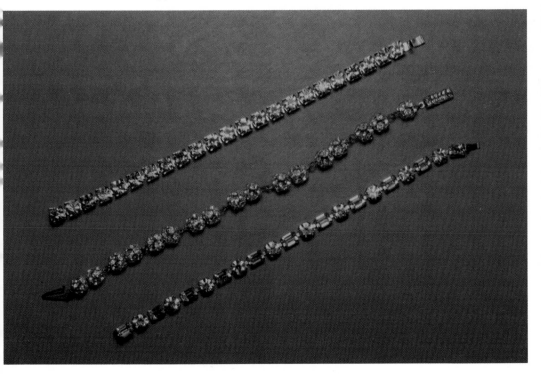

Of these three bracelets, the center one is marked Made in Czechoslovakia. Its detail is outstanding. Bracelets $35-95.

Round and emerald faceted stones are used in the pin while bracelet is of square facets. Pin $35-50. Bracelet $35-60.

These pieces utilize various shaped stones. Pin is convertible to pendant. Earrings $25-40. Pin $20-30.

Light and airy sprays. Lower pin is signed *V.D. Sterling* and top pins are marked Austria. Pins $30-50.

Geometric design is used in this hinged bracelet and pin from the 1960s. Pin $20-35. Bracelet $30-50.

Pin is typical 1940s, signed *Garne Jewelry.*
Bracelet is one of a million made in this
simple style. Pin $50-75. Bracelet $25-45.

The earrings are signed *Eisenberg.* The
pins are unsigned with marquise cut stones
to match the earrings. Earrings $65-85. Pins
$40-60.

Pyramid design of pin and straight lines of
earrings create a dramatic pairing. Both
pieces are unsigned. Earrings $20-30. Pin
$85-100.

Pave set stones with baguettes enhance
this *Trifari* pin. The necklace uses the same
combination in a much simpler style. Pin
$60-95. Necklace $40-55.

Dainty bracelet with pave set stones compares favorably to other pieces pictured here. Surprisingly, none are signed. Pins $35-50. Bracelet $60-80.

The pin of this set is much older than the earrings. Each incorporates drops for added effect. Earrings $25-45. Pins $75-100.

Collection of smaller pins and dress clips all done in pot metal with glued in stones. Pins $20-35.

Complementary use of design and stones. Bracelet is signed *Weiss*. Earrings $20-30. Pin $20-35. Bracelet $65-90.

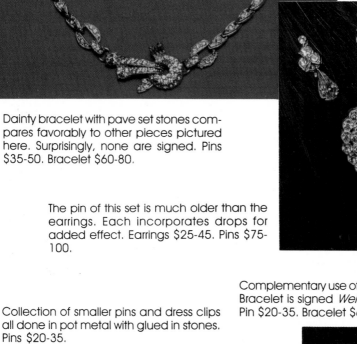

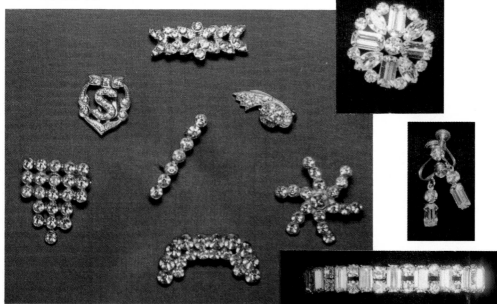

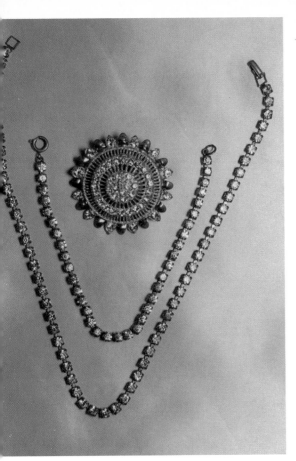

Older brass-like metal is used in these pieces. Nothing spectacular but very wearable. The bracelet is marked Czechoslov on the O-ring. Pin $35-55. Bracelet $25-45. Necklace $35-50.

Round and emerald cut stones add to this elegant tiered necklace and earrings. Earrings $20-35. Necklace $65-95.

This 2" stunner demands attention. Note the center dip. Bracelet $125-150.

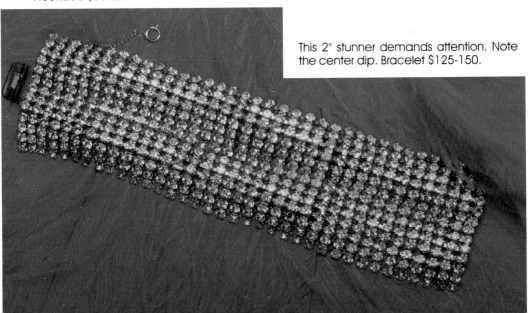

Common use of round rhinestones make up the center pairs of earrings. The outer 3" earcoverings are designed to hook over the top of the ear. Earrings $20-95.

A type of duette that is worn as a pin or separated into two fur clips. The bracelet is signed *Natty Creations* and, after many guesses, was determined to have held a dress train of the day. Duette $95-125. Bracelet $175-210.

Unsigned necklace and earrings using round and pear shaped stones. Found in its original box which had deteriorated with time. Set $60-75.

The center earrings are signed *Bogoff*. All use the clear rhinestone theme for elegance. Earrings $40-75. Bracelet $60-95.

Chapter 14

Figurals

Figural - "likeness or representation of a person or thing"

Designers' imaginations gone wild created these pieces that are fun to wear and bound to be a topic of conversation. What fun they must have had, as we did photographing them!

Our apologies to all of the crafts people out there, but this is the only kind of costume jewelry Christmas tree we want to see! The following pieces are signed: Row 1 - Santa *B.J.*; Row 2 - left is *Lisner* and the right is an H inside a heart; Row 4 - left is *B.J.*, center is *Hollycraft*, and right is *Art*. It should be noted that the earrings to the Hollycraft tree above are unsigned. Pins $35-75. Set $75-105.

None of these wonderful bows are signed. The bottom one is a copy of one done in true gemstones. Pins $35-75.

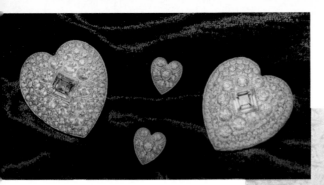

Romantic hearts all belonging to the Author's mother for many years. The earrings are stamped Sterling. Earrings $35-50. Pins $50-75.

Colors you would never see in nature but brilliant and unusual. Set $50-75.

Spanning many years, these Christmas pins are a joy of the season. The dog is signed *Mylu*, the horn is signed *Coro*, and the bell is signed *Art*. Pins $40-100.

Held gently in one's hands, this vibrant butterfly is signed *Regency*. Pin $95-125.

Birds of a feather flock together in these three pairs of scatter pins. Pairs $30-55.

All these older pieces are very well made with great care and attention shown to detail. The center pin with aqua and blue crystals is marked Czechoslovakia. Pins $75-110.

Ready to fly off the page, this unsigned pin is done in enameling and clear rhinestones. Pin $100-125.

Flocking to the flower, these bugs are remarkable. From the large dragon fly to the trembler winged bee, to the red and brass bug marked Czechoslov. Pins $65-125.

Exactly the same except for stone colors, these two flamingos flank their feathery friend. Pins $75-95.

Flower set uses frosted round cabochons to separate the dainty enamel and rhinestone flowers. The bird is marked Austria. Pin $30-45. Set $45-65.

Enameled metal flowers of springtime colors with pale yellow rhinestones for sparkle. Set $50-75.

A tisket, a tasket, flowers in and out of baskets. The basket pins are marked Made in Czechoslovakia. Pin $45-75.

Seen in many other publications, we chose to focus on the dragon's head. *HAR* does have an imagination! (also seen in white). Bracelet $225-285.

Slithering quartet of snakes with green rhinestone eyes. Pin $75-95.

Snakes to charm the money out of your pocket. *Art* scores big with this unusual and detailed four piece set. Set $275-350.

Two styles of earrings using the same colors. Both are clip type and unsigned. Earrings $25-65.

Incorporating enameling and rhinestones set in gold metal, these pins create a flowery display. The center pin and earrings also use colored crystal beads. The horseshoe shaped pin on the right is marked Austria. Pins $20-55. Set $40-60.

Nature's apple blossom branch and its costume jewelry interpretation. Summer hat is signed *BSK* and *My Fair Lady*. Pins $45-70.

Amphibians and reptiles sharing a "pad." The turtle on the left is a trembler with reverse set stones for the head and feet. The turtle on the right is signed *J.J.* The frogs are scatter pins. Pins $25-105.

Sarah Coventry's signature appears on all these pieces done in aurora borealis set in gold metal. Pins $50-65. Set $65-85.

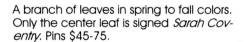

A branch of leaves in spring to fall colors. Only the center leaf is signed *Sarah Coventry*. Pins $45-75.

The trembling pearl center of this unsigned flower attracts a swarm of bees. Pin $100-125. Scatter set $40-65.

Larger pin has 3-D flowers with pink rhinestones on the inner petals and enameling for stems and leaves. Smaller pin is actually a fur clip. Pin $65-95. Clip $45-65.

Gold metal and clear rhinestones still make for clean lines, be it flowers or bugs. Pins $20-65.

Exceptional floral pieces of days gone by. Dark blue piece is marked LN/25. Pins $85-125.

Art, in their creative style, depicts an eagle with enameling, pearls, and a deep green rhinestone eye. Pin $100-125.

Signed *Trifari*, this fur clip is a 4" bouquet of enameling and pave set rhinestones, demonstrating superior workmanship and detail. Clip $175-225.

Signed *La Roco*, the butterfly is a multitude of colors. The earrings appear to repeat the wing pattern. Set $95-110.

Symbols of our country from Betsy Ross sewing the flag, to the bicentennial pin, to the GOP mascot. Pins $25-75.

All pieces are unsigned in this simulation of butterflies flitting around a flower. Pin $35-50. Set $55-75.

No kennel could hold this pack of pooches. It should be noted that the black poodle is by far the oldest. Pins $20-95.

Out for a walk with man's best friend, this pin is unsigned. Pin $50-75.

Dancers attached by a double chain can be worn in many fashions. Pin $50-75.

Mary, Mary, Quite Contrary's garden would never have been the same had she had these beauties. The two center flowers are signed *Weiss.* Pins $65-105.

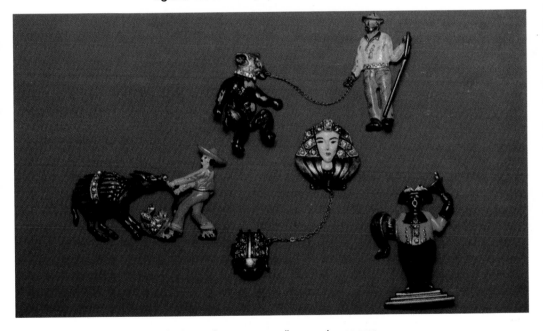

All pieces have enameling and a sparse use of rhinestones in common. The similarity ends there! Cleopatra with her ever present scarab, the trainer and his dancing bear, the stubbornest of mules, and a town crier. Each proving the designers had a lighter side. Pins $150-250.

Sunflowers and daisies are dominated by opaque marquises. Earrings are signed *Weiss*. Earrings $35-50. Pins $30-45.

Could the other earrings have a matching flower pin like the peach set? Matte enameling over gold metal with matching rhinestone centers. Earrings $20-30. Set $30-50.

Dainty butterflies float above a flowered trembler that comes to life when worn. Pin $65-95. Pair $20-30.

Spray your fruit trees or you could end up with these bugs. However, we welcome this sort of pest. Pin $45-65. Pair $25-45.

Spawning decades, we have a school of
fish on an ocean of color. Upper right fish
with green cabochon eye is signed *J.J.*
The large silver pin is actually a bird eating
a fish. Pins $30-75.

Can you find all six feathered friends in this
"duck blind?" Pins $20-50.

Pair of enameled birds in flight, with clear rhinestone accents, soar above the unusual fur clip grasping a large faceted blue stone. All are unsigned. Clip $100-125. Pair $50-75.

An artist's palette could have painted all these creatures. Multicolored bird is signed *Weiss* and the horse is marked Czechoslovakia. Pins $25-75.

Framed fruits. The apple and pear pin is marked Austria, the strawberries are *Weiss*, and the blue berries are *Hollycraft*. Pins $45-95.

Signed *Joseff* on the bottom of each "cage," these cherubs swing to and fro. Bracelet $175-250.

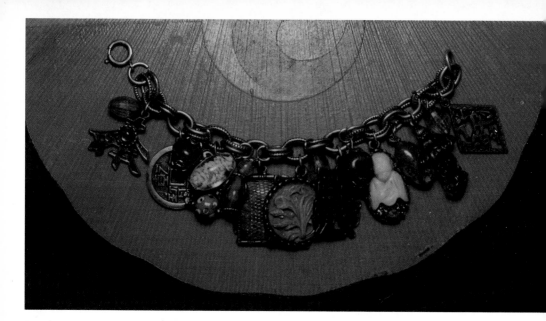

This unique charm bracelet, in the oriental style, combines several mediums. From metal, to plastic, to glass, and finally rhinestones. Though unmarked, we are relatively certain it was done by Napier. Bracelet $95-145.

Fur, leather, and rhinestones. What a combination! Pins $25-50.

Chapter 15
Accessories

Accessories - "something added to help in a secondary way"

Representative of just how rhinestone crazy people got, making the dullest, everyday objects sparkle!

Accessories using rhinestones were only limited by the imagination. These rhinestone studded gold tubes hide an array of practical tools including toothbrushes, a pen, and a zipper pull. Accessories $25-45.

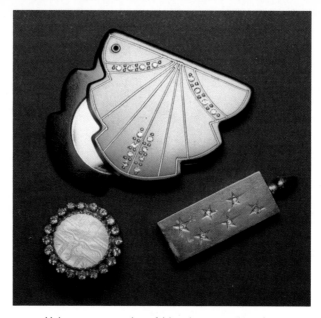

Yet more examples of rhinestone madness!
A mirror that swings open and closed, a
perfume bottle, and a pill box with carved
mother of pearl surrounded by rhinestones. Accessories $40-65.

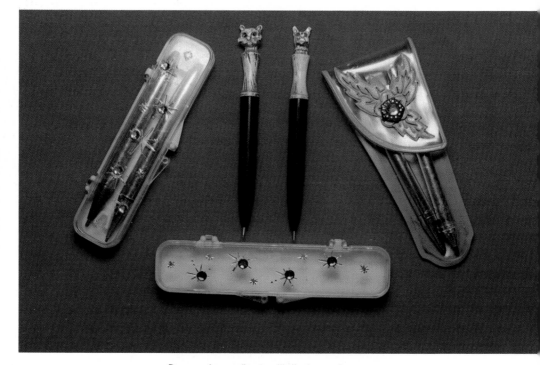

Pen and pencil sets with their carrying cases
are all accented with rhinestones. Sets
$20-30.

The pin pal by *Hallcraft* was used to hold scatter or stick pins. The dogs (resembling the Author's American Eskimo Husky) sport blue rhinestone collars. Pin Pal $35-50.

A notebook with rhinestone clasp, fleur de lis bookmark with aurora borealis, rhinestone decorated pen, and an amber rhinestone accented *Swingline* stapler all prove even simple writing tasks can be fun. Accessories $20-45.

Assortment of rhinestone lipstick holders, with the bottom two signed *Wiesner of Miami*. The center piece is a mirror that clips to a lipstick case. Accessories $40-80.

Florenza not only created jewelry but vanity accessories as well. The bottom is a pin cushion/box and the top is a lipstick holder. Both are signed. Accessories $55-95.

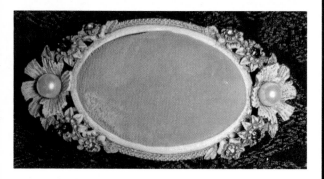

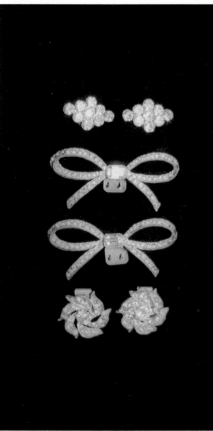

Add these sparkling clips to your dullest shoes and change your look from day to night in an instant. Clips $20-45.

Only a small sampling of the essential compact. All use different mediums including opaque black glass stones, mother of pearl, rhinestones, and pearls. Lower right has a clear *Judy Lee Jewels* tag on the back. Compacts $40-65.

A good overview of belt buckles done in clear and colored rhinestones. The center piece has large blue faceted glass stones and both are signed *WMAC* and stamped with an R. The right piece is stamped with an arrow through a box. Buckles $45-120.

Every rhinestone in this adjustable length belt is the same size and is prong set. Eight triple dangles, including the clasp, add to the design. Belt $85-125.

This gold metal purse is 5.25" x 3" in size. The front is of cork set into a frame of mother of pearl decorated with shells, rhinestones, pearls, seahorses, and a hungry octopus. The inside contains a compact, lipstick space, fabric change purse, and a metal mirror hiding a storage or cigarette compartment. Purse $75-150.

Entirely of prong set rhinestones sewn together, this 7" x 5" bag is lined in cream colored satin with an inside pocket and zippered closure. Purse $90-140.

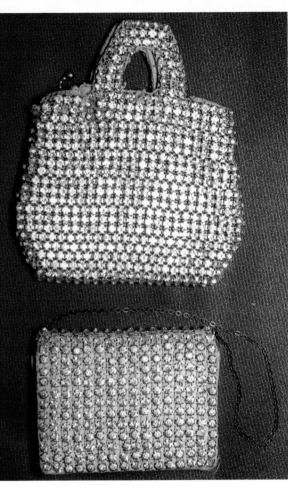

Both of these rhinestone over file purses have been well used and enjoyed. The lower foldover example also contains a small mirror in its own case. Purses $90-140.

This wallet encrusted with colored rhinestones and pearls has its original box with a book reviewing European art and fashion. The book states "The House of Noah has brought to American shores in *Daniel Creations* the ultimate in beauty." Wallet $50-75.

Half a dozen sweater guards in different styles used to hold a sweater when worn over the shoulders. Sweater guards $20-40.

Rhinestone studded *Schiaparelli* sweater
can either be worn with a poodle skirt and
the sunglasses by day or for a more serious evening cover-up. Glasses $25-45.
Sweater $85-115.

Rhinestone trimmed gloves kept together
by the also rhinestone glove holder. Gloves
$25-40. Glove holder $20-35.

A multitude of rhinestones cover the three sided true hat pin with a 9" shank. The hat decoration uses square stones for its design. Hat pin $75-115. Decoration $35-55.

Though having seen many night spots, there is still a lot of life left in these *Qualicraft* rhinestone heels of the past. Shoes $100-150.

Even though they say rings are hard to find, you would never know it by this display. The top row, left to right, are signed *Florenza*, *Emmons*, *Emmons*, and *Florenza*; the rest are done in a rainbow of colors. It should be mentioned that in the second row, the ring second from the left is stamped Germany. Rings $45-150.

Five rings from bottom to top: emerald shaped blue rhinestone, three bands with green rhinestones, five bands with blue rhinestones, rainbow stones in nickel silver, and a dome signed *Sarah Coventry*. Rings $20-50.

Many rings in many colors. All are prong set and unsigned. Rings $20-50.

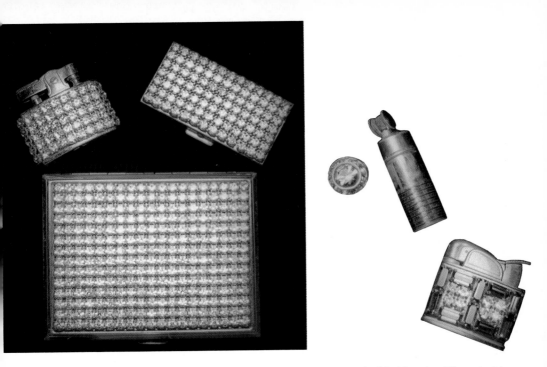

Typical of the many vanity and smoking accessories that were done in gold metal and covered with rhinestones. Shown here are a pillbox, cigarette case, and lighter which is signed *Trickette by Wiesner*. Accessories $65-125.

Two bejeweled lighters in different styles. The traditional lighter with purple stones is signed *Evans*. Lighters $40-75.

A trio of ashtrays, two are glass with rhinestone rims and a poodle at the side. The square box is a purse version. Ashtrays $25-50.

Signed *Volupte USA*, the enameled cigarette case is simply decorated with flowers accented by rhinestones and pearls. Case $75-100.

Two exceptional barrettes in a free-flowing style. The "bird" is stamped France. Barrettes $40-65.

An assortment of hair barrettes, clips, and bobby pins, all using the rhinestone theme. The far left and center clips are signed *Lady Ellen*. Accessories $25-50.

More hair decorations in plastic and rhinestones. These can be worn singularly or as a pair. Decorations $20-40.

Sold in pairs, these hair decorations all have rhinestones to accent your "Do." Pairs $20-40.

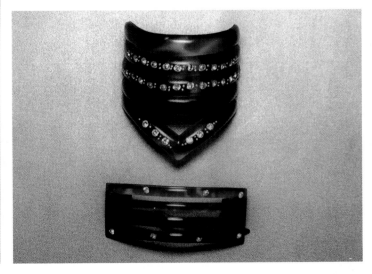

Two barrettes done in faux tortoise shell and clear rhinestones. Barrettes $20-45.

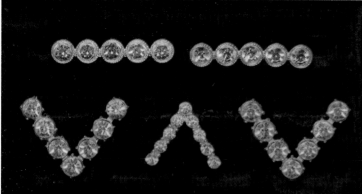

Sewn on decorations to accent any outfit. Decorations $15-30.

Stunning hair combs of pink and lavender marquises centered by an aurora borealis stone. The flowers are spring-hinged onto the comb. Combs $65-100.

From older to newer, these hair combs hold a lady's crowning glory. Combs $20-50.

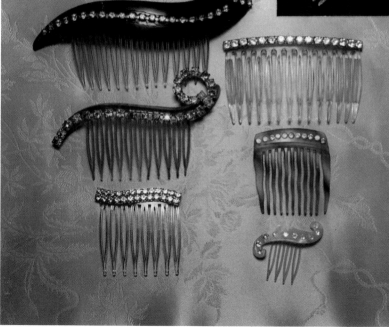

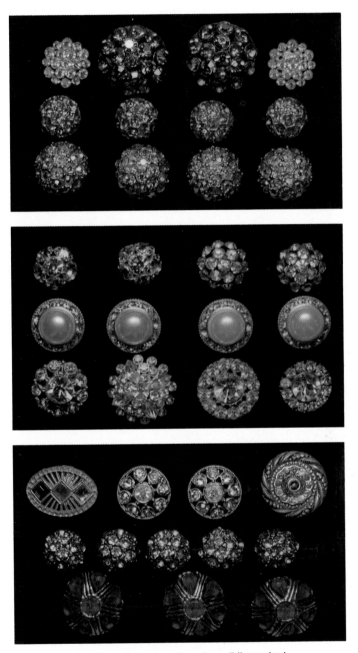

From simple to spectacular, all these buttons have one thing in common, RHINESTONES! We've been known to buy a piece of vintage clothing just for the buttons. Buttons (each) $5-25.

Not even candlesticks could escape the rhinestone treatment. These 10 inchers of brass could grace any table setting. Candlesticks "special".

Even time pieces utilize rhinestones. The pink boudoir clock has complimentary pink stones and is by *Westclock*. The *Bradley* travel alarm clock uses clear stones to mark the hours. Clocks $35-75.

Two jewel accented perfume atomizers whose bulbs have long since disintegrated. The pink 6.5" is marked „Made in Germany West on an applied circle. Atomizers $45-90.

Bibliography

Baker, Lillian. *Fifty Years of Collectible Fashion Jewelry 1925-1975*, Paducah, KY: Collector Books, 1986/1989.

Ball, Joanne Dubbs. *Costume Jewelers The Golden Age of Design*, West Chester, PA: Schiffer, 1990.

Dolan, Maryanne. *Collecting Rhinestone Jewelry, An Identification and Value Guide*, Florence, AL: Books Americana Inc., 1989 and 1993.

Ettinger, Roseann. *Popular Jewelry 1840-1940*, West Chester, PA: Schiffer, 1990.

Ettinger, Roseann. *Forties & Fifties Popular Jewelry*, Atglen, PA: Schiffer, 1994.

Kelley, Lyngerda and Schiffer, Nancy. *Costume Jewelry The Great Pretenders*, West Chester, PA: Schiffer, 1987.

Miller, Harrice Simons. *Official Identification and Price Guide to Costume Jewelry*, New York, NY: House of Collectibles, 1990.

Miller, Harrice Simons. *Costume Jewelry Identification and Price Guide*, New York, NY: Avon Books, 1994.

Schiffer, Nancy. *The Best of Costume Jewelry*, West Chester, PA: Schiffer, 1990.

Schiffer, Nancy. *Costume Jewelry: The Fun of Collecting*, West Chester, PA: Schiffer, 1992.

Schiffer, Nancy. *Fun Jewelry*, West Chester, PA: Schiffer, 1991.

Schiffer, Nancy. *Rhinestones! A Collector's Handbook & Price Guide*, Atglen, PA: Schiffer, 1993.

Index

About the Authors

Sandy Fichtner was raised in the Shakespearian theatre community of Ashland, Oregon.

Her captivation with rhinestone jewelry began at an early age when her mother would bring out the treasured jewelry box filled with family mementos. The sense of family has always had a strong influence on her life and these rhinestones were handled like diamonds because of their origin, "Grandmother had actually worn these glittering pieces of the past!"

A collector by nature, Sandy loves her costume jewelry, vintage clothes, and all that goes with them.

Lynn Ann Russell was born and raised in Media, Pennsylvania, and attended Elizabethtown College, receiving a B.S. degree in biology.

Although standing only 4'11", there is nothing small about her personality or her passion for life. Her earliest memories of costume jewelry are sitting at her Great Aunt Fran's dressing table playing in the "junk jewelry" drawer. Now she collects rhinestones with a passion. She also spends many hours creating beautiful cross stitch pieces for her family and friends.

Inquiries can be made to the authors at P.O. Box 1621, Cave Junction, Oregon, 97523.